Trail-Hunting, Rabbiting and Ratting with Hounds and Terriers

A Modern Approach to Traditional Hunting

by
J C Jeremy Hobson

Published in 2014 by Skycat Publications
Vaiseys Farm, Brent Eleigh, Suffolk CO10 9PA
Email info@skycatpublications.com
www.skycatpublications.com

ISBN 978 0 9927451 2 7

Printed by Lavenham Press
Arbons House, 47 Water Street, Lavenham, Suffolk CO10 9RN
Telephone: +44 (0)1787 247436
Email: enquiries@lavenhamgroup.co.uk

© 2014 J C Jeremy Hobson

All rights reserved. No part of this book may be reprinted or reproduced or utilised in any form or by any electronic, mechanical or other means now known or hereafter invented, including photocopying and recording, or in any information storage or retrieval system, without permission from the publishers in writing. In accordance with the Copyright, Design and Patents Act 1988, J C Jeremy Hobson has asserted his right to be identified as the author of this work.

Any description of hunting outside the restrictions of the Hunting Act which came into force in February 2005 must be understood to have taken place before its inception.

The information contained in this book is true and complete to the best of our knowledge. All recommendations are made without any guarantee on the part of the author or publishers, who also disclaim any liability in connection with the use of this data or specific details.

The source of photographs is credited alongside the image: where there is no credit shown, these are the author's own.

Jacket cover photos:
Front cover:
Top left: Greg Knight (ruralshots.com)
Top right: Barry Isaacson
Middle left: Greg Knight (ruralshots.com)
Middle right: Author's own
Bottom left: Author's own
Bottom right: Greg Knight (ruralshots.com)

Back cover:
Greg Knight (ruralshots.com)

About the Author

JEREMY HOBSON is a freelance professional author and writer with a lifetime's interest and knowledge of all aspects of hunting. He was a whipper-in to a pack of beagles in his teenage years and has followed all manner of hound packs, both mounted and on foot. He has also judged at hound and puppy shows.

Before turning to writing as a full-time profession twelve years ago, Jeremy was, for over three decades, a gamekeeper concerned with both grouse and pheasant and, during the course of that work, kept several working terriers. Throughout his career, he has written countless articles and 30 books – including Beagling (David & Charles, 1987) and Working Terriers (Crowood Press, 1989).

Jeremy Hobson nowadays lives in France (a country where hunting and hounds are still revered!) where he continues to follow the French packs and visit the various hunting-related shows as often as time and locality allows.

Other books by J C Jeremy Hobson

Dogs & hunting
Beagling — David & Charles
Working Terriers — Crowood
Gundogs: your problems solved — Batsford

Shooting & gamekeeping
Small-scale Game Rearing — Crowood
Gamekeeping — Crowood
What Every Gun Should Know — David & Charles
Cultivating a Shoot — David & Charles
Running a Shoot — Crowood
The Shoot Lunch — Quiller
A Practical Guide to Modern Gamekeeping — How To Books
Sporting Lodges: Sanctuaries, Havens & Retreats — Quiller

Smallholdings & livestock
Successful Smallholding (co-authored with Phil Rant) — Crowood
Keeping Pigs (co-authored with Phil Rant) — David & Charles

Poultry & chickens
Bantams: a Guide to Keeping, Breeding and Showing — Crowood
Backyard Poultry Keeping — Crowood
Backyard Ducks and Geese — Crowood
Keeping Chickens (co-authored with Celia Lewis) — David & Charles
Keeping Chickens (2nd, revised, edition) — David & Charles
Choosing and Raising Chickens — David & Charles
Èlever des poules — Terres éditions
Success with Chickens — Quiller
Keeping Chickens (3rd, revised, edition) — David & Charles

Country cooking & cookery
Cook Game — Crowood
The New Country Cook — Crowood
Chutneys, Pickles and Relishes — Crowood
The Rabbit Cook — Crowood
The Pigeon Cook — Crowood

Rural living & country interests
Rural Living in France — Survival Books
Curious Country Customs — David & Charles

Miscellaneous
The Lost Poems of W. H. Kennings (ed) — Blackwell Printers

Author's note

It is important to note that, wherever possible, I have tried to avoid using inclusive pronouns (e.g. "his or her" and "he and she") in the text: sometimes though, for pure convenience, I have used "he" as a neutral pronoun and absolutely no sexist inference should be taken from this.

Also, unless specifically stated, the reference to any company, organization, product or publication in this book does not constitute an endorsement or recommendation.

Contents

Acknowledgements

Preface

Introduction   1
Now and Then; Anti-hunting Groups; How Today's Situation Came About; Hunting within the Law – a simple classification for rabbits and rats; The Legalities of Gun-packs; Defining Trail Hunting; Fostering Goodwill; What's in a Name?; The Social Media

Hounds and Terriers   15
Bassets – Griffon Vendeen, Fauve de Bretagne, Bleu de Gascogne, Artesian Normand, English; Beagles; Foxhounds – trail hounds; Bloodhounds; Dachshunds; Terriers – Airedale, Bedlington, Border, Cairn, Dandie Dinmont, Fox, Jack Russell, Lakeland/Fell, Manchester, Norfolk and Norwich, Plummer, Scottish, Sealyham, Sporting Lucas, Welsh, West Highland, Wheaten, Yorkshire; Colouring and Coats; Size Matters!; Desirable Attributes – in hounds – in terriers; Undesirable Faults; Pedigree, Pure or Pooch?; Make-up of a Bobbery Pack; Naming Hounds and Terriers – terrier titles, puppy christenings

Hunting with Others   59
Hunting Seasons; Who Goes Hunting?; Making Contact – a note for secretaries; Where the Meet is Held; At the Meet – some do's and don'ts; How Many Hounds? – how many terriers?; Hunt Staff – the huntsman, masters, whippers-in, the "quarry" and trail-layers; On the Trail; The Situation Overseas

Sport with Your Hounds and Terriers   77
Livestock – don't endanger your dog; Teaching Dogs to Jump; Entering Hounds and Terriers – hounds, entering hounds to an artificial line, terriers, aiding education, the age to begin, awakening the "prey drive", training terriers to hunt and quarter; Keep Calm and Carry On; Hunting Rabbits with Hounds and Terriers – optimise your opportunities, learning from the experiences of others; Scenting and Weather conditions – weather conditions affecting hunting; "View Holloa!"; Urban Hunting – the Connaught Square Squirrel Hunt

Kennels, Health and Hygiene   95
Kennels and kennelling – temper tantrums; Transport; Exercise –

hounds, terriers; Feeding; Health and Hygiene – ticks, mites and allergies, leptospirosis, kennel cough, injuries and wounds, poison problems, snow affecting the pads of hounds and terriers; Vaccinations; Organic and Herbal; Some Notes on Breeding – selecting the right stock, general observations; Whelping and Puppy-care; Tail Docking; Tattoos – micro-chipping legislation

What to Wear   117
Coats and Jackets – one for the ladies!, "camo" gear; Shirts and Underclothes; Breeches and Trousers – waterproof leggings; Overalls and Kennel Coats; Boots and Wellingtons – boot bags; Hats, Gloves and Scarves; Hunt Uniforms; Bags and Rucksacks

Useful Equipment   127
Specific Ratting Gear; Collars, Leads and Couplings – a word about electric collars; Whips and Things – making a "cracking band"; Horns and Whistles; Pocket Knives; Ideas for a First-aid Kit – a first-aid box for humans; Keeping Notes; Binoculars'; Cameras'

Summer Shows and Socialising   141
Puppy Shows; Hound Shows – a useful tip; Showing Terriers – to their best advantage; Terrier Racing; Hound Trailing; Game Fairs and Country Shows – dogs left in cars at shows: Clay Shoots and Barbeques – hosting a successful one; Hunt Balls; Social Events as a "Thank You"

Glossary   153
Further Reading   157

Acknowledgements

FIRST and foremost, thanks must go to Debbie Jackson and Ali Myer at F&W Media International Ltd, for granting permission to use some material which first appeared in my book *Beagling* (published in 1987 by David & Charles).

I am also extremely grateful to Mrs Daphne Thorne of the Barony Bassets; her kindness and willingness to answer my questions and share with me her experiences of setting up a rabbiting pack is greatly appreciated – as is her promptness in replying to my emails. Thanks too, to the masters, huntsman and members of the Old Berkeley Beagles ... as friendly a bunch as one could ever wish to meet.

As far as photographs are concerned, I would very much like to thank Greg Knight of Rural Shots (www.ruralshots.com) for both his friendship, and his kindness in agreeing to provide me with some of the excellent photos used in this book. To take good photographs, one needs a thorough understanding of the subject matter – and, fortunately for me (and many more of his "fans" – particularly on Facebook); Greg has this in bucket-loads! Others who have helped immensely in supplying images are: John at Darswed Teckels; Janine Evans; Robert Latham and Gemma Baron. Special thanks must also go to Darren Clark for the hound-trailing photos and to Barry Isaacson for the Rookley Rabbit Dogs photos. The latter images came as a result of the assistance of Liam Thom of Liam's Hunting Directory and I much appreciate his help.

Some pieces of general information are an amalgam of my own knowledge and casual conversations had between huntsmen, masters, terrier owners and rabbiting and ratting enthusiasts over recent months. As much for my own pleasure as for finding out information, I've had some lovely days out with several hound packs. I've also gleaned many thoughts and opinions from experienced terrier-men – both in person and via various Facebook groups. Their un-named input was invaluable – as were the efforts of various people who have assisted by suggesting leads and possible contacts: amongst whom I include Lynn Pawley (of *Hound Trailing News*).

I should just point out that, in accordance with my understanding of the UK's copyright laws, I have not necessarily sought permission to quote minor extracts taken from book, magazine and Internet where they amount to merely a few words – and can assure anyone concerned that I have not taken the quote out of context. I have, on every occasion, also acknowledged the source/publication alongside. In other instances I have made every effort to ensure that permission has been sought. Should, however, anyone reading these pages feel that is not the case, I can only offer my apologies, together with the promise that, if they will be kind enough to get in touch with me via the publisher, or directly through my website (j-c-jeremy-hobson.co.uk), I will most certainly make amends in future reprints.

Preface

AS FAR as hunting foxes and hares with hounds are concerned, the Hunting Act 2004 radically altered traditional hunting. The Act is, though, quite bizarre in that it continues to allow the hunting of rabbits and rats with packs of hounds and terriers – provided, of course, that one has the landowner's permission. In late 2013, suggestions were made that it might be possible to amend the existing Act so that more dogs might be used in the pursuit of foxes; this was mentioned as being of likely benefit to upland sheep farmers.

No matter what the eventual outcome of any amendments and reforms might be, there has, nonetheless, always been an interest in a group of like-minded friends taking out a mixed "pack" of terriers, whippets and nondescript dogs for a little Sunday morning excursion after rabbits and rats. Quite often it was a regional thing – such sport at one time possibly being most prevalent in the north.

If anything, the (current, at the time of writing) restrictions of the Hunting Act has made the pursuit of rabbits and rats even more popular – with the result that there are today, several packs who have created a more organised approach to what was often a casual last-minute affair generally organised by a few friends during a sojourn in the local pub the previous evening! Known by some as a "bobbery" pack, the name is thought to be Far East in origin and is probably a corruption of the Hindu "Baap Re", used to describe the practice of hunting various species of quarry with a group of hounds made up of differing breeds and types.

J E Marriat-Ferguson, writing in his 1905 classic *Visiting Home*, tells of the makings of a bobbery pack built up by himself and fellow officers when stationed in India during the 1880s: " 'Curly' Knox had brought with him a couple of harriers from England, old Astley had a couple and a half of lurchers which he'd bred himself from a greyhound and a fox terrier … and I added to the confusion by buying a useful-looking dog of no obvious parentage from the man who sold fish to the Officer's Mess. Together we made quite a hullabaloo as we crashed after jackals … a poor substitute for fox hunting in Hampshire, but a diversion from the daily duties!"

Then there are the official packs of foxhounds, beagles and basset hounds – some of which have actually been formed since the Hunting Act – which are registered with the Masters of Foxhounds Association (MFA), the Association of Masters of Harriers and Beagles (AMHB), or the Masters of Basset Hounds Association (MBHA). Carefully regulated so as to not fall foul of any legislation, these packs might perhaps most commonly be used to follow an artificially laid "trail". Their "meets" are certainly more formal than those of the casual groups who gather to follow a melange of bobbery hounds and the packs have meet cards printed for the season, as well as thriving supporters' clubs that organise various social (often fund-raising) events throughout the year. The hunt staff dress in recognisable attire and operate under long-established "rules" of etiquette.

No matter how enjoyable an afternoon following hounds following an artificial scent might be, I think that most would admit that trail-hunting with hounds does not have the same element of spontaneity and uncertainty and there are many purists who want to watch hounds work against a wild quarry in a natural manner. To all intents and purposes, where it can be legally carried out, this type of hunting is as traditional as any ever was and whilst in the case of what were originally hare-hunting packs followed on foot, there might not be the spectacle of fine horses and immaculately turned-out followers, there is always a die-hard and enthusiastic following. In addition, there is also the fact that one is performing a "service" to landowners and the like. Daphne Thorne, Master of the Barony Bassets, says that she finds that, "farmers, landowners and shoot owners welcome rabbit hounds and are grateful for the modest amount of pest control we carry out – anything from nought to fifteen rabbits in a day. In places where they really want numbers reduced we have some followers who are only too happy to bring their ferrets along and supplement the tally."

There are pest control firms using sporting breeds of dogs in places where poisons and/or firearms would be neither safe nor suitable. One, based in the south, claims that they pride themselves on "working some of the best dogs in the industry" and "use various breeds, from terriers to lurchers depending on the location and nature of the job. Where rabbits cause a problem in dense cover we employ terriers and spaniels to flush rabbits into long-nets. Terriers fitted with a tracking system can also be used to clear rabbits from tunnel systems such as wire ducts, as well as from under buildings."

Even when out for pleasure on a simple country walk, we all know the fun to be had from watching a dog as it hunts a rabbit up and down a hedgerow. The quick movements when it scents the rabbit, the thorough questing when it has lost it, and the excited cry when it comes close to the rabbit and running in view. It is, therefore, also possible for rabbiting and ratting with hounds and terriers to be either a solitary one, a work mission, or enjoyed in the company of a few friends and their dogs as one "mooches" along hedgerows and ditches over land on which one has permission.

Before I end this Preface, I should just point out that rabbiting and ratting with sight-hounds such as whippets and lurchers is a very different entity and I have made a conscious decision not to include too much mention of that particular sporting activity. There is, however, inevitably a certain cross-over (a bobbery pack may, for instance, include the odd lurcher as well as hounds and/or terriers) and so, hopefully, those who mainly enjoy such days out will also find much of interest between these pages. As evident from the book's title, there is also reference made to trail-hunting – a very necessary inclusion for many reasons – and I trust that those who pursue this aspect of field sports will find those particular sections of benefit and value.

Happy Hunting!
J C Jeremy Hobson
2014

INTRODUCTION

IN MY YOUTH, I used to love reading the tales of the Bagley Rat Hounds which appeared regularly as articles in the *Shooting Times* during the early 1970s. Penned by the somewhat eccentric Jack Ivester Lloyd, they were enough to fuel the enthusiasm of a young teenager with a couple of terriers, his grandfather's collie cross, and time on his hands!

Jack Ivester-Lloyd was well-known as being "master" of the Bagley Rat Hounds which he used to hunt around his home in Shropshire. He was also a tremendously well-respected writer and author, passing on his knowledge and enthusiasm for hunting and country matters through his work. Indeed, Brian Plummer (a popular writer on dogs and matters sporting, as well as hunting with his own bobbery pack; being instrumental in the development of the modern Sporting Lucas terrier, and creating the Plummer terrier

Fig 1: Hare-hunting with the Colne Valley Beagles in the early 1970s. Photo: Janine Evans

breed) wrote in his book *Diary of A Hunter*: "My gloom is dispelled by a letter from Jack Ivester Lloyd praising my book *Nathan*. Praise from a writer of his ilk is praise indeed."

Ivester Lloyd was also a keen beagler and, as I'd been a follower of our local beagle pack (the Colne Valley Beagles) from a very early age, I read and re-read his classic 1954 book, *Beagling*, gaining some new insight each time I did so.

At that time, beagling concerned itself with the pursuit of hares but, since the Hunting Act 2004 (which actually came into force in February 2005) the situation has changed somewhat and, later on in this chapter, there is a brief yet pertinent section appertaining to "hunting within the law".

NOW AND THEN

The bizarre situation that allows hunting rabbits, but not hares, with hounds has resulted in several new packs being formed; amongst them, in Scotland, the Barony Bassets and, in England, the Caldew River Rabbit Hounds. Others, such as Nick Valentine's Ryeford Chase rabbit hunting hounds have been around for some years prior to the 2004 Hunting Act.

The way "private" packs of hounds operate can, at times, be very reminiscent of the days long-gone when wealthy land-owners had their own pack of foxhounds or harriers kennelled in the grounds of their estate. In other instances, some of the possibly less formal privately organised "packs" whereby a group of friends come together with their own hounds and terriers for a few hours of exciting sport, are similar to the times when several people kept a couple or two of hounds at home and then brought them together for a days' hunting. Known as "trencher-fed" packs, they were particularly popular in the Lakeland fell districts.

Such sporting activities are not, however, always confined to the countryside and I was very interested to recently read of a particular ratting pack which was formed to hunt in the urban back ally-ways of New York's Manhattan. Known as the Ryders Alley Trencher-fed Society (RATS), the pack of "hounds" includes Border terriers, a wire-haired dachshund, a Jack Russell/Australian cattle dog cross and a Patterdale – and has, apparently, been the scourge of the city's rat population for over a decade.

Although there can be no doubt that this motley crew of dogs are an effective form of vermin control, Richard Reynolds – who might in other circumstances be referred to as the master and huntsman – says that it's as much about "maintaining the breed type through actual work". Apart from the unusual environment in which they operate, in all other respects, the way this pack hunts is not all that far removed from those of a similar nature which eradicate rats around farms and in the British countryside. But, believe it or believe it not, even rat-hunting like this is not immune from the attentions of the anti-hunting lobby. PETA (People for the Ethical Treatment of Animals) apparently expressed outrage when it learnt of the New York rat-hunting brigade and a spokesman referred to it as being "a twisted blood sport masquerading as rodent control".

ANTI-HUNTING GROUPS

With the unbelievable thinking and bizarre comments of PETA in mind (see above), it might just be worth making brief mention here of the history and development of certain anti-hunting groups in the UK.

Probably the first organised opposition to hunting came with the formation of the Humanitarian League in 1891. Although founded by two RSPCA members, Messrs Salt and Williams, it was not primarily concerned with anti-hunting matters and, in 1924, two former members of the League, Messrs Amos and Bell, felt that neither the league nor the RSPCA were doing enough to turn the public against hunting in general. As a result, they formed the League for Prohibition of Cruel Sports – which is now known as the LACS (League Against Cruel Sports). The year 1963 saw the foundation of the Hunt Saboteurs Association, a subsidiary of the LACS and founded by members who intended to disrupt hunting by less passive methods than mere placard-carrying. Their plan was fourfold: first to keep the organisation informal, second to concentrate on disrupting hunts, third to encourage other animal welfare organisations to press for a legislative change, and fourth to remain just within the law.

The RSPCA still seem intent on decrying fieldsports in general and traditional hunting in particular. In the summer of 2013, they called for countryside groups to join forces and create a new, independent trail and drag-hunt association (see also *Defining Trail-Hunting* later in this section). Gavin Grant, the RSPCA's chief executive at the time, proposed that if such groups were prepared to sign up to a new self-regulating association, it would have the support of the charity and he implored landowners to only allow access on their property to members of such an association. Mr Grant's proposals were, understandably, dismissed by many – including the Countryside Alliance. Sir Barney White-Spunner, executive chairman

Fig 2: An early anti-hunt protest under the name of the LACS. It is uncertain whether the woman in the centre is a lone protester – or is accompanied by the man talking to the trilby-wearing gentleman on the right.

of the CA summed up the mood of most knowledgeable country-dwellers and true fieldsports enthusiasts in saying: "We are quite happy to talk to the RSPCA in the interests of animal welfare when the RSPCA drops its increasingly radical and politicised animal rights agenda."

HOW TODAY'S SITUATION CAME ABOUT
Once the Labour party had a big majority, a ban on fox-hunting was always on the cards. The party's power base has generally tended to be very much an urban one, with a rather low understanding of anything that goes on in the countryside. It has, of course, always had a class bias and it is not hard to understand how hunting would be (erroneously) considered an upper class preserve – "the unspeakable in pursuit of the uneatable" as Oscar Wilde so famously put it so many years ago. Not long after Labour was voted back in power in 1997, parliamentary pressure was put – primarily by Sports Minister Tony Banks. Tony Blair and his more cautious political advisers

knew that hunting was likely to be nothing but trouble long-term and, has subsequently been revealed in Blair's autobiography, *A Journey* (Arrow, 2011) he did everything he could to delay things. Nonetheless, as Donough O'Brian's book, *Banana Skins* (Bene Factum Publishing, 2006) pointed out: "The shocking and ridiculous fact is that 100 times more parliamentary hours were spent on hunting than were taken up with the rather more important matter of Britain's attack on Iraq."

HUNTING WITHIN THE LAW

Since the Hunting Act 2004, how, what, where and why one might hunt has changed. Dry reading though it may be, it is probably as well to lay out some of the most relevant points in relation to rabbiting and ratting with hounds and terriers. Basically the Act:

> "… prohibits all hunting of wild mammals with dogs in England and Wales, except where it is carried out in accordance with the conditions of one of the exemptions set out in the Act. It also bans all hare coursing.
>
> The Act makes it an offence for a person to hunt a wild mammal with a dog unless the hunting is exempt. For the purposes of the Act, the word "hunting" has its ordinary English meaning, which includes searching for wild mammals, chasing them, or pursuing them for the purpose of catching or killing them. The Act makes clear that a person is hunting a wild mammal with a dog if he engages alone or participates with others in the pursuit of a wild mammal and a dog is employed in that pursuit, whether or not under his direct control. As hunting requires the intention to search for, chase or pursue the quarry, it is not possible to hunt by accident.
>
> The Act also makes it an offence for a person knowingly to permit land which belongs to him to be entered or used, or to permit a dog which belongs to him to be used, in the commission of an offence of unlawful hunting."

It is, though, the exemptions that we need to look at in a book that concerns itself greatly with rabbiting and ratting with hounds and terriers:

> "… The Act sets out several classes of exempt hunting under which dogs may be used to hunt wild mammals, subject to strict

conditions. Exempt hunting must always take place either on land which belongs to the hunter or which he has been given permission to use for that purpose by the occupier or, in the case of unoccupied land, by a person to whom it belongs.

Dogs may be used to hunt rats or rabbits, to retrieve a hare which has been shot, or to flush a wild mammal from cover to enable a bird of prey to hunt it. Up to two dogs may be used to stalk or flush out a wild mammal if the stalking or flushing out is carried out for one of the following purposes: preventing or reducing serious damage which the wild mammal would otherwise cause to livestock; to birds or other property; or to the biological diversity of an area; participation in a field trial in which dogs are assessed for their likely usefulness in connection with shooting.

The stalking or flushing out does not involve the use of a dog below ground unless the requirements of the "gamekeepers' exemption" are complied with …"

Basically, the "gamekeepers' exemption" is as follows:

"A single dog may be used below ground to stalk or flush out a wild mammal if:

The stalking or flushing out is undertaken for the purpose of preventing or reducing serious damage to game birds or wild birds which are being kept or preserved for shooting; the person doing the stalking or flushing out carries written evidence of land ownership or the permission of the owner or occupier. This evidence must be shown to a police constable immediately on request."

In addition, the following conditions must be adhered to:

"Reasonable steps are taken to ensure that as soon as possible after being flushed out from below ground the wild mammal is shot dead by a competent person; the dog used is brought under sufficiently close control to ensure that it does not prevent or obstruct the shooting of the wild mammal; reasonable steps are taken to prevent injury to the dog; and the dog is used in compliance with any code of practice which is issued or approved by the Secretary of State for the purpose of this exemption."
Source: Defra

Simple clarification for rabbits and rats
The hunting of rabbits and rats is exempt provided it takes place on land that variously: belongs to the hunter; he has been given permission by the occupier or, in the case of unoccupied land, by the landowner. There is no limitation on the number of dogs that can be used. However, should there be any question about the legalities of a particular instance; subsequent investigations will consider the following:

> "Was there evidence that the hunted wild mammal was a rabbit or rat? Was there evidence that any other (non-exempt) wild mammal was hunted? Did the hunting resemble any pre-ban hunting activities – for example, in the case of where rabbits are the supposed quarry, does the pattern of hunting resemble that of traditional live quarry hunting (hares run for extended distances in open fields whereas rabbits tend to make short dashes to their warrens)?
>
> If any other wild mammal, which is not exempt, was pursued was there any evidence that the dogs were called off? Was there evidence that the dogs were encouraged to hunt the wild mammal, for example with the use of horn and/or voice calls?"

THE LEGALITIES OF "GUN-PACKS"
Whilst the main aim of this book is to talk of hunting rabbits and rats with hounds and terriers, in order to be as complete as possible with regards to certain legalities, it perhaps ought also to be mentioned here, the use of both hounds and terriers as they are (and were), used by gun-packs to flush a fox to a line of waiting guns.

In 2000 (before the 2004 Hunting Act), a submission to the Committee of Inquiry into hunting with dogs had this to say: "… from records over the last few years, [it is] estimated that, for a Welsh gun pack using hounds to drive foxes towards waiting shotguns, around 15-20% of foxes were wounded and not killed outright ... [However] the majority will be caught since hounds are available to follow up and kill wounded foxes."

To remain within the law as it currently stands, in most instances (but with the exception of Scotland where a full pack can be used to flush foxes provided that they do not then continue to hunt in open ground), one can only use two dogs to push foxes towards waiting guns (see *Hunting within the Law* above). This two-dog exemption was originally included within the Hunting Act mainly to address a problem that farmers and landowners

Fig 3: Since the Hunting Act, there are many restrictions on the way foxes may be hunted. In addition, badgers have been protected in most of the UK by the Badger Act of 1992.

could face in controlling foxes and was accepted by anti-hunting MPs as being a "utilitarian necessity". As Jim Barrington, animal welfare consultant to the Countryside Alliance commented in 2013, "The trouble is it doesn't work, so it is only right that the Government reviews that aspect of the law and amend it to enable that exemption to achieve its intended aim."

In October 2013, the Federation of Welsh Farmers Packs (FWFP) called for the existing Hunting Act to be amended so farmers are allowed to use a full pack of hounds to flush a fox to a gun. They called for the change as a result of research carried out in Scotland on their behalf the previous winter. The information gleaned suggested that "using a full pack of hounds can be

Fig 4: Since the introduction of the Hunting Act, many packs, both mounted and on foot, have adapted well to the sport of trail-hunting.

twice as effective as using two dogs". The Countryside Alliance supported the move in principal but added that "any amendment must not be seen as an alternative to the full repeal or replacement of the Hunting Act". Downing Street even commented by saying that, "There is a very specific issue here around pest control and the impact it has on particular farming communities such as hill farmers."

However, until such reforms – or even a full repeal – we do, at the time of writing, still have to adhere to current legislation, a part of which includes trail-hunting either on horseback or on foot.

DEFINING TRAIL-HUNTING

Although the unofficial bobbery packs operating a service to farmers and landowners (and, of course, having some good fun and sport in the process) will hunt only rabbits and/or rats, and several of the private basset packs only rabbits; many of the registered beagles and basset packs more often than not concentrate on laying down an artificial trail for hounds to follow.

In the course of an afternoon, distances can mount up and, as an example, on the Albany and West Lodge website, it is stated that their bassets will frequently hunt over some 25 miles whilst the huntsman may well cover 15 and the whippers-in 10.

It might help to define the difference between trail-hunting and drag-hunting; the latter being excellently described by Charles Armstrong in *British Hunting* (edited by Arthur Coaten) in which he opined that drag hunts were originally started by serving Army officers who sought amusement, or by "gentlemen engaged in commerce" who had not enough time to hunt properly but relished a cross-country gallop with hounds. He then went on to say that, "This class of hunting differs materially from the pursuit of any animal inasmuch as the course is previously mapped out, on the principle of a steeplechase."

It is well worth noting here that according to the website of HuntingAct.org, when the 2004 Hunting Act came into force, the Masters of Draghounds and Bloodhounds Association (MDBA) "were particularly concerned that illegal live quarry hunting, under the guise of following an artificially laid scent, would have a detrimental effect on the sport of drag hunting. Therefore, in order to prevent their sport being brought into disrepute, the MDBA insisted that the term 'drag hunting' remained their exclusive property. As a consequence the term 'trail hunting' was invented."

Unlike drag-hunting, the main point of trail-hunting is not to get from A to B in as quick a time and as straight a line as possible, but is intended more to simulate a natural path that would be taken by a wild animal such as a fox or hare as it attempts to evade its pursuers. To that end, the artificial line will be laid to double back on itself, pass over natural and artificial obstacles, and cross a variety of terrain.

Fig 5: Few of us would have any hunting at all if it wasn't for the generosity and good nature of sporting farmers, landowners and shooting tenants.

Whatever the differences between drag and trail-hunting, one thing on which enthusiastic followers of either must agree is on the point raised by Charles Armstrong where he says that there would be no such thing were it not for the generosity of sporting farmers who not only make their land available, but often throw in a splendid "hunt breakfast" as well.

FOSTERING GOODWILL

I make no apologies for continually mentioning the fact that, as few of us are lucky enough to own our own estate, hunting of any type would not exist without the co-operation of landowners and farmers. It is, therefore, crucial that there is mutual goodwill and sporting enthusiasm in equal measure.

For the individual seeking permission to pursue rabbits and/or rats on a particular farmer's land, a careful, studied approach is necessary. Here are some thoughts to consider when cold-calling in search of "permission".

* *Remember that, quite rightly in these days of increased rural theft, farmers can be suspicious of "cold-callers".*
* *A lot of farms are shot over by game shooting syndicates and the like – and so any vermin control will most certainly be carried out during the "close" season by their members, keeper and/or regular shoot helpers such as beaters.*
* *Make it clear that your dogs are well-trained and livestock-steady and that you are only interested in working them on rabbits and/or rats.*
* *If possible, be able to produce references which say you are trust-worthy in such situations.*
* *Look smart and presentable – first impressions do count.*
* *Learn to accept that, if there are no sporting opportunities on a farmer's land, there is probably a good reason for this – there is absolutely no point in trying to persuade such a person otherwise and you will only alienate them.*

Assuming that you do eventually obtain permission, it is as well not to abuse it by taking out various like-minded friends without first of all asking. Knowing the Country Code (and, more importantly, abiding by it) is crucial and, should you notice anything seemingly amiss on the farm, it is as well to report it straight away. An offer of help to the farmer outside the "season" (moving livestock, bale-carting et al) – plus a bottle of spirits or case of wine at Christmas will also go a long way towards fostering goodwill.

Hound packs have always understood the importance of goodwill and cooperation with landowners, farmers and gamekeepers. It has long been the traditional responsibility of a master and/or huntsman to visit such people during the summer months in order to ensure that the country over which hounds hunt is kept open to them. Such visits are essential, particularly when planning a meet card as, although some will not mind when hounds visit, others would prefer that it is not during the shooting season or, if conducted outdoors, during lambing time.

An organised pack will also make sure that none are neglected when it comes to invites being issued to such things as the annual puppy show and many will hold a Farmers' Dinner towards the end of the hunting season – to which farmers, landowners and their keepers are "guests of honour". Such occasions are the perfect way of spreading the word and ensuring perfect co-operation in the future. It works both ways – a really clever hunt organiser could do far worse than invite local gamekeepers to be, not only "guests of honour", but also cajole one of them into being an after dinner speaker. An articulate gamekeeper can then use the opportunity to explain to the hunting folk present, just exactly what their work entails.

Mind you: should you be approached, it's not a date to be entered into your diary lightly. When someone asks you at the end of October, for instance, to speak at an event next February or March, it might seem an easy request and be light years away but, let me tell you, having succumbed to such pleas in the past, as the date approaches, it becomes an ever more daunting prospect!

WHAT'S IN A NAME?

Whilst many of the packs registered with the AMHB and MBHA have names associated with the area and country in which they hunt – and it's not unusual for private packs to be known by the name of their owner – there seems no reason why anyone connected with an unofficial bobbery pack of hounds, lurchers and terriers shouldn't call themselves by whatever name they choose. In the past there has, for instance, been the Meon Valley Rat Hounds (sadly now defunct after giving some two decades of glorious sport), the Bromyard and District Rat Hunt and, as mentioned at the very beginning of this Introduction, the Bagley Rat Hounds under the "mastership" of Jack Ivester Lloyd. As I write, there are in existence, several with the suffix of "Rabbit Dogs", "Rabbit Hounds" and the like (photos and details of which can be seen on the Internet) plus many more informal ones of which no-one bar the participants and local supporters are aware.

As to whether there is any criteria to be followed before naming one's pack of hounds or terriers, I cannot really see why there would be – if you are using your name, or the name of your property there should certainly be no problem. Using the name of a geographical area might, though, be a different proposition and my suggestion would be to check and see whether there is a similarly named registered pack listed in Baily's: it would probably not do much for hunting entente cordiale if you gave your "pack" a name that appears remotely like any existing hunt.

Understandably, those associated with the more formal set-up could well have very reasonable concerns regarding the existence of another similar sounding pack over which they have no control or jurisdiction. As to whether you can name your pack after your local village, I would suggest contacting the clerk of your parish council and seeing what they have to say on the matter.

Going off ever so slightly at a tangent, one contributor to an online hunting forum opined that "… those who operate 'unregistered packs' on whatever scale, and with whatever types of hounds, lurchers, terriers and …other dogs might prefer that their names, locations … and so forth remain the subject of idle speculation …" In saying as much, there is, perhaps, the underlying suggestion that some unregistered packs put together by groups of enthusiastic hound and terrier workers may have something to hide. To avoid such speculation in the future, it is the responsibility of anyone and everyone involved in rabbiting and ratting activities, whether registered with the various associations or not, to ensure that all their hunting activities are legal and above board.

Fig 6: The Rookley Rabbit Dogs hunt on the Isle of Wight. Photo: Barry Isaacson

THE SOCIAL MEDIA

There are, very sadly, many who would have hunting of almost any description outlawed. For some their opposition is due to ignorance and preconceived ideas, while others perceive the very word "hunting" to be associated with an "upper-class" activity. Whereas we all know that nothing could be further from the truth and that the majority of us who enjoy such sport are most certainly not in that exalted position, it is an image that many refuse to consider otherwise. We must, therefore, treat all our days out as if we are being watched and do nothing whatsoever to bring hunting (in all its guises) into disrepute.

On occasion, our activities are actually being watched, particularly when it comes to the social media networks such as Facebook. Although some groups are "closed" to all but members, it is still relatively easy for those who wish to stop any kind of hunting with working hounds and terriers to see what comments and photos are being posted. Whilst all the time that doing so is legal, there is nothing to hide – but why risk providing ammunition for the anti's in the shape of photographs taken of lines of dead rabbits and rats or, in situations where it is legal to do so, of foxes taken by terriers? A comment posted on the Facebook site of one particular group showed that there are very conflicting thoughts on the subject – at least judging by these observations made in response:

"Hide nothing, I say ..."

"We have to be shy of what 'they' might use."

"Most don't agree with those kind of pictures ... get rid of them, it doesn't do us any favours ... I am not ashamed of what I do but I don't feel the need to show it off."

"Yes, anti's can search for stuff and use the pics for propaganda but they can also hide in hedges or use cameras."

"Pics are ok but maybe some are a tad too graphic?"

"Try to avoid 'blood and guts' ... otherwise I don't see that it is wrong – many may object to it for various reasons but that's life."

"I don't know how useful the attitude/tone that seems to accompany some of these pictures is."

So there we are; there's very definitely some "food for thought" amongst that particular selection of comments. Please consider them carefully before posting anything that might be at all controversial on any form of social media.

HOUNDS AND TERRIERS

AS I MENTION elsewhere, many hounds have a traceable lineage and pedigree more easily investigated than most humans, and it is quite safe to say that all of the recognised and registered packs have, over generations, developed a type which suits them; the country over which they hunt, and the scent (artificial or otherwise) most likely to be encountered. For others, though – the "bobbery" packs and ratting terrier aficionado – we have to ask what breed or type of dogs are the best and most commonly used. I suppose one could say that provided it is of the right temperament and "drive", any type will suffice but generally, it is the hounds and terriers that interest us most within the context of this book.

BASSETS
French in origin, the basset (meaning low-set or dwarfed) originally developed as several distinct types. Nowadays, however, only four main varieties exist – two smooth-coated and two rough-haired – and these are the Griffon Vendeen, Fauve de Bretagne, Bleu de Gascogne and Artesian Normand. Whilst some may argue the point, it is generally accepted that their forebears resulted from a genetic freak in the sixteenth century when some puppies of normal-sized French staghounds began to develop retarded limbs. In all other respects they were normal and, human nature and curiosity being what it is, these small hounds were kept by several interested persons and mated together until they began to breed true to type.

Today's working bassets are a delight to observe out hunting. They are determined, both physically and mentally strong and, once they are on the scent, are not at all deterred by thick cover, difficult terrain, or any distraction from either livestock or hunt followers.

Above: Fig 7: Bassets are French in origin.
Below: Fig 8: Today's working bassets are a delight to observe out hunting. Photo: Greg Knight (www.ruralshots.com)

In addition, the typical basset gives tongue more readily than some other types of hound and, no matter what the particular breed type, will speak on a scent in such a way that it can make the hairs stand up on the back of your neck. Even Shakespeare referred to the noise of what surely must have been basset hounds in *A Midsummer Night's Dream* where he has Theseus saying; "Their heads are hung/With ears that sweep away the morning dew'/Crook-knee'd and dew-lapt like Thessalian bulls/Slow in pursuit, but matcht in mouth like bells." Nick Valentine, owner and Master of the Ryeford Chase hounds (quoted in a *Country Life* article), also mentioned the fact that the sound of bassets in full cry were like something one might hear from a church tower on a Sunday morning when he remarked that; "I love standing in a field listening to them going off like a peal of bells."

Griffon Vendeen

There are actually four types of Griffon Vendeen hounds used in France (the "Grand" – for deer and boar; the "Briquet" – for deer and fox; the "Grand basset" – for hare; and the "Petit" basset – for hare and rabbit hunting). In the UK, it is the latter two that are seen in connection with the type of hunting under discussion in this book and, of the packs put together with the express purpose of hunting rabbits in a formal and traditional manner, Petit Griffon Vendeen bassets seem to feature prominently. The Barony Bassets which hunt in southern Scotland is made up of this type – due partly to the fact that Daphne Thorne, who started the pack, "used to look at the picture of petit griffon basset vendeens in Sir John Buchanan-Jardine's book *Hounds of the World* and long for a pack of them." Another hunt that consists of Vendeens is the pack belonging to Tom Langshaw which hunts twice weekly along the tussocky growth and grasses of the foreshore between Stranraer and Glen Luce. The Caldew River Rabbit Hounds which hunt in the north-west of England, is however, a mixed pack of Griffon Vendeen bassets and beagles.
*(**Note:** Although I refer in the text mainly to "Petit Griffon Vendeen bassets", others, including the Kennel Club, mention "Petit Bassets Griffon Vendeens" and so, where they have, I have written it exactly as it has been given to me.)*

Fauve de Bretagne

Ian Cunningham, who was, for almost three decades, Master of the Pevensey Marsh Beagles, decided to form Mr Cunningham's Rabbit Hounds after the

2004 hunting ban came into being. Like those mentioned above, his pack contains Griffon Vendeens, but also a few Fauve de Bretagne.

George Johnston, writing in *Hounds of France*, is of the opinion that the current breeding is (in France at least) a result of enthusiasts in Brittany who crossed the few remaining Fauves of the time with Griffon Vendeen bassets and "… possibly, red-coloured wire-haired dachshunds". As Johnston remarks, "The cocky swagger and carriage is certainly indicative of a dachshund outcross." He also opines that their movement is certainly not "the quick, twinkling gait of the Artesian Normand or the bold, proud action of the Griffon Vendeen".

Prudence Gravillons, an Irish woman married to a French wine-grower living in the Bordeaux region, has a small pack of three and a half couple

Fig 9: Fauve de Bretagne bassets.

of Fauve de Bretagnes which she regularly works over their land and maintains that the breed is "perfect for hunting rabbits and give excellent sport". Prudence also says that individuals of the breed can be jealous and undisciplined but, on the plus side, "are unbelievably courageous in the thick cover that immediately borders my husband's vine fields".

Bleu de Gascogne

As with the Griffon Vendeen, there is a foxhound-sized type of Blue de Gascogne and both this and the basset are named after the region of France in which they originated – and for the colour of their coats, which are generally described as being blue "ticked". Perceived wisdom has it that the basset variety originated from the larger hound, as a result of cross-breeding with this and other shorter-legged varieties. The unusual and attractive colouring is thought to occur from a natural mutation in the combined genes.

Apart from the coat colours, the physical appearance of the dog is believed to have been developed sometime after the French Revolution when it became permissible for the lower orders of French inhabitants to hunt – a privilege which had, up until then, been the sole prerogative of the king, counts and other landed gentry. As the more ordinary person didn't possess the types of horses traditionally used by wealthier members of society on which to indulge their passion for hunting, the basset was a perfect hound as it was slower and could be followed on foot.

By the beginning of the twentieth century, the future of the Bleu de Gascogne was not looking so good and it was Frenchman Alain Bourbon who mated three bitches of the even rarer Basset Saintongeois

Fig 10: A young basset of the Bleu de Gascogne type.

breed with a large Bleu de Gascogne sire and, by a process of selection, eventually produced the type of Bleu de Gascogne basset seen on today's hunting field. In 1911, Bourbon commented that: "For the old huntsman riddled with gout or rheumatism preventing him hunting "a-courre", it is with a few couples of these little hounds that he will rediscover his youth!"

Artesian Normand
This type of dog is the one that would be most commonly recognised by the lay-man as being a "Basset hound" and is of the colouring and make-up similar to the animal used as the marketing tool of the makers of "Hush Puppy" shoes. Sadly, the extraordinarily elongated body, unnaturally long-eared, wrinkled-faced, "Queen Anne" legged example used there (and also seen in the show ring and on the street), bears hardly any resemblance at all to the true working basset known either as the Artesian Normand or the English basset (see immediately below).

Nowadays commonly seen and hunted in countries other than France, the breed has been used to cross with the Hush Puppy type basset and many packs contain examples with a mixture of both types in their make-up.

Fig 11: The type of basset hound most recognized by the general public!

Fig 12: A wagging stern and alert head are the trade mark of all hounds no matter what their breed!

English Basset

Rather than give it a totally separate heading, I am intentionally including what is often referred to as the "English" basset here as an addendum to the vaguely similar looking Normand. As to their development, it is interesting to note that the pack now known as the Westerby were originally the Walhampton Bassets which hunted in the New Forest until their owner, Godfrey Heseltine, moved to Lutterworth, Northamptonshire in 1920. Together with his brother Geoffrey, Godfrey founded his Walhampton pack in 1891 with freshly imported hounds from France.

After Heseltine's death in 1932, the name was changed to Westerby and, according to Internet information, a Dr Morrison subsequently "experimented with various outcrosses before and after the war, ultimately having the most success with a stud book harrier in 1950 from which the present pack is descended, thus establishing the so-called English Basset. Since then there have been further infusions of pure basset, harrier and West Country harrier blood."

The renewed interest in bassets resulted not only in the reforming of the Basset Hound Club in 1954 but also an extension of their objectives in the form of a working branch. From this arose the Albany pack which was also Kennel Club registered.

While on the subject of "English" bassets, Daphne Thorne mentions that the reason she chose Petit Griffon Vendeen bassets when setting up her pack in 2006 was because of the fact that when she whipped in to the Test Valley about 40 years ago, she was "rather put off English bassets by the amount of fighting that took place in kennel". The hounds were, however, drafts, so maybe they were drafted because they were aggressive. As Mrs Thorne says: "I blame no-one for their behaviour, but it was rather heart-breaking."

BEAGLES

Even though it is the Hunting Act that has forced such things upon us, there is nothing new in hunting rabbits with beagles. In 1946, Roger Free, author of *Beagle and Terrier – their training and management at home and in the field*, suggested that a small pack of them would "have the advantage of being absolutely tireless in their pursuit of the elusive rabbit and add to the day a touch of colour and music that would otherwise be missing".

A century earlier Blaine, in his *Encyclopaedia of Rural Sports* published in 1840, refers to several types of beagle; two of which were the wire-haired (probably descended from the Welsh hounds) and the smooth-coated. By 1873, the breed had become recognised by the Kennel Club and it seems that the pocket beagle was also beginning to attain certain popularity. They were never more than 10 inches (25.5cm) high and eventually bred true to type. In one book of the era, it was noted that "… the late Col Hardy had once a collection of this diminutive tribe amounting to ten or twelve couple, which were always carried to and from the field of glory in a pair of large panniers slung across a horse".

Nowadays, the type of beagle seen either following an artificial trail or out rabbiting, are the same as those which had, previous to the Hunting Act, been used to hunt hares for many, many years. As is the case with foxhounds, hunting beagles have a lineage that can be traced back for generations – more so, in fact, than most human dynasties!

Whilst still on the subject of beagles, it might be worth pointing out that the Hunting Act does not affect the majority of Ireland and, as a consequence, there are packs of beagles that hunt both fox and hare which are recognised by the Hunting Association of Ireland. In addition, keeping alive the old tradition of "trencher-fed" packs, there are several small groups of men and women who keep two or three beagles each and come together in order to hunt regularly. Likewise, there are also many lurcher and terriermen who keep a beagle in their kennels; the idea being that it will run a fox to ground for their terriers, or bolt one from cover to lurchers positioned around the perimeter.

Fig 13: Beagles waiting for the off!

HARRIERS

Whilst no-one (to the best of my knowledge) uses harriers out rabbit hunting, there are several recognised packs throughout Britain, all of which follow a trail. Before the Hunting Act, their quarry was, however, the hare and/or fox. These packs are healthy and thriving and quite contradict the thinking of Rawdon Briggs Lee who, in 1879, was of the opinion that: "Unless some very considerable change takes place, it is extremely likely that the harrier will not survive very many generations, at any rate in this country. His type has not been strictly defined for years, he has varied much in height, and has lately been crossed with the foxhound to such an extent as to further endanger his extinction."

Thankfully, Rawdon Briggs Lee's predictions were proved wrong and there are nowadays, two distinct breeds of harrier: the stud book harrier and the West Country harrier. According to the AMHB, "the stud book harrier is smaller and lighter than the West Country harrier".

Interestingly, and long before Lee recorded his observations, that great huntsman Peter Beckford wrote of his harriers as being a cross between the large slow hunting southern hound and the beagle. They were, according to contemporary accounts, fast enough, had all the alacrity desirable, and would hunt the coldest scent. These attributes gave them an ability to hunt

Fig 14: Apart from size, harriers and foxhounds are generally quite similar in appearance. Photo: Greg Knight (www.ruralshots.com)

with "plodding perseverance" – unlike some other harrier packs of the time which were apparently too fast for the hares they hunted.

FOXHOUNDS

The foxhound packs of mainland Britain had, in the main, no option but to turn to trail-hunting after the Hunting Act and whilst trail-hunting is by no means the main subject of this book, the fact that it is included means that so too, should be foxhounds – particularly when it comes to fell-trailing, of which more in *Summer Shows and Socialising*.

Foxhounds in general need no description. Like the beagle, whilst the colouring might vary, their overall appearance is the same. Unlike the modern-day beagle, it is, however, possible for the coat to be wiry as is the case with the Welsh foxhound. Nonetheless, having made the rather sweeping statement that, apart from colouring, all look remarkably similar, one foxhound type that many may fail to recognise is the fell-hound which has been used for generations on the hills, crags and scree of the Lake District.

Hunted on foot, fell hounds are rangier in shape than a foxhound from the shires and are, in the main, lighter in colour in order that their whereabouts can be seen by the huntsman from far away. It is these types of hounds that have been instrumental in the make-up and development of the trail hound – and the main reason why I have included foxhounds in this section.

TRAIL HOUNDS

Trail hounds were originally bred from foxhounds out-crossed with the likes of pointers, harriers and even sheepdogs in order to develop a faster hound with a good nose. Eventually, the trail hound recognised today evolved and they have been bred true to type for many generations with only the occasional rare influx of foxhound blood.

Bred for stamina and speed, trail hounds are similar to greyhounds in that they are raced competitively with bets being placed on the outcome. Unlike greyhounds, they follow a scent with their noses rather than an artificial lure with their eyes. They also run/hunt over terrain varying from low-lying pasture to steep fell sides with streams, walls and ditches to be crossed in-between rather than around a track.

Fig 15: Trail hounds are of slighter build than other hounds and are bred for stamina and speed. Photo: Darren Clark

BLOODHOUNDS

In order not to be accused of neglecting to include all types of hounds that might be used in trail-hunting of one form or another, it is important to mention, if only briefly, the bloodhound. Unlike the rest which hunt an artificially laid trail comprising of various concoctions and solutions, bloodhounds hunt the "clean boot" – the scent of a person who runs ahead of the pack a short while before they are loosed.

Bloodhounds are surprisingly fast given their slow and ponderous appearance when in kennels or out on exercise and following one of the recognised and registered packs can be quite an illuminating and exhausting experience! The runner (quarry) is first of all acquainted with the hounds allowing them to recognise his scent before then setting off on a pre-determined course and given about a thirty minute start. As Jeremy Whaley, master and huntsman of the South Downs Bloodhounds notes within his website, "Unlike hounds following a laid trail, the natural scent of a human being is different from person to person and is easily affected by weather

Fig 16: Bloodhounds hunt the "clean boot" rather than a laid artificial scent.

conditions ..." Whilst the route the quarry takes is always agreed with the landowner/farmer in advance, there is, as the website says, "frequently enough latitude within the route for an experienced quarry to carry out a variety of manoeuvres to try and outwit his pursuers. Thus the pace, and even the successful conclusion of a hunt, will depend on the skill of the huntsman and his hounds."

DACHSHUNDS

Although it was bred to hunt by scent and then follow its quarry underground, the dachshund is generally recognised as being a "hound" and so I thought it correct to include it here. Who knows, someone out there might one day consider creating a rabbiting pack of the "standard" size wire-haired type. There are two sizes in the UK, the standard weighing around 20-26lbs (9-11.5kg), and the miniature at about 10-11lbs (4.5-5kg). Three coat types include the smooth, long and wire-haired). Although most run mute when hunting – unless the scent is particularly strong, or they can see the quarry (see Jack Ivester Lloyd's observations immediately below), I would guess they ought to provide good sport.

Working dachshunds in their home country of Germany are variously called "dackels" or "teckels", but in the UK and elsewhere, many people draw a distinction between the dachshund and teckel – the latter being a wire-haired working type not infrequently used by deer stalkers to follow-up on a wounded deer.

Jack Ivester Lloyd, "master" of the Bagley Rat Hounds, was of the opinion that you couldn't do better than include a dachshund or two in a bobbery pack and noted that, from his personal experience, "dachshunds work in exactly the same way as a basset hound, have the same nose for a cold line and throw their tongues in the same manner." He also said that, whilst one of the terrier members of his pack was "inclined to be 'flashy' [and would] often draw over a squatting rabbit … the older dachshund never does this. His long, pointed nose misses nothing [and] as soon as the dachshund's deep voice announces that a rabbit is on its feet, the terrier streaks to him, knowing what has happened."

Fig 17: A brace of working teckels (Darswed Teckels).

That dachshunds might be a valuable asset to modern-day hunting can further be evidenced by the writing of Sir Jocelyn Lucas, author of *Hunt and Working Terriers*, in which he recounted that a keen hound man had once volunteered to sell him a pack of miniature dachshunds which were supposedly small enough to go down almost any rabbit-hole and drag out whatever might be in there. In America, field trials are held for dachshunds in much the same way as they are for beagles and bassets and if, during the course of a trial, a rabbit runs into a tunnel or drain large enough for the dog to enter, it is expected to do so without hesitation or the need for encouragement.

TERRIERS

Most of the terrier breeds in existence today were developed for their ability to work underground after fox, badger or otter and it is probably only the Airedale, Bedlington and Manchester terriers that were bred specifically for rabbiting or ratting – not that almost any of the breeds mentioned wouldn't make a useful addition to a "bobbery" pack out and about!

Airedale

Appropriately for a book of this nature, the Airedale – which was originally known as the Waterside or Bingley terrier before being credited with its present name – was derived by sportsmen in this area of Yorkshire to hunt out rats and other vermin from the slopes of the Aire Valley. It is larger than other breeds of terrier (and is known by some, particularly in North America, as being "the King of Terriers", both for its size and personality) and most individuals will work well alongside any of the smaller breeds. The true working strains are not at all fazed by cover and will enter and hunt through some of the thickest places.

Bedlington

As far back as 1702, gypsies living near Rothbury in Northumbria were using a type of dog "with coats like lambs" in order to hunt hare and rabbit. In the 1860s, the Cowny family of Morpeth had Bedlington-type dogs which they used for rabbiting and ratting but the facts surrounding the actual development of the breed are a little hazy. The original "Rothbury" terrier was, perhaps, at some stage, crossed with the whippet and the Dandie Dinmont in order to produce a dog which, as one particular website has it, "was cheap enough to feed, hard enough to tackle rats in the local factories or steel foundries and fast enough to catch a rabbit." Arguably nowadays more often seen in the show ring than out working (although Bedlingtons are a popular lurcher cross), the Working Bedlington Forum might be of interest to those hoping to seek out true working strains (http://www.workingbedlington.co.uk/index.php).

Fig 18: Bedlington terriers were once described as having "coats like lambs'. Photo: Gemma Baron)

NB: *Briefly mentioned above as often being crossed with various suitable breeds to make very useful working lurchers, there is at least one person in the UK who hunts rabbits and rats with a small pack of Bedlington cross French basset hounds: others could do much worse than consider such a mating.*

Border

The Border terrier is a popular generally useful breed, but originally it was bred specifically to be both agile and brave enough to take a fox. It also needed to have sufficient stamina to enable it to run all day with hounds and even today, the breed standards stipulate that it should "be capable of following a horse". With the possible exception of its head and muzzle, the general overall appearance has not changed all that much for well over a century and it is still possible to recognise certain characteristics of the modern Border in pre-WWI photos of its ancestors.

One particular breeder and worker of Borders says that they are "intelligent, loyal, biddable and great with children ... Personally, I have not found them difficult to train but you do need to put the work in early on and be consistent ..." Perhaps it is because of these attributes that the breed is extremely popular nowadays: a decade and a half ago, there were only around 900 registered with the Kennel Club whereas in 2014, the number is more like 7,000 – and Border terriers account for 25 percent of the total dogs registered with the KC each year.

Fig 19: Working Border terriers from the first decade of the 20th century

Cairn

In West Yorkshire during the late 1960s, I knew of a man who used to successfully hunt rabbits on the borders of low moorland with five Cain terriers, and have since also seen several instances of such dogs being used for a bit of unofficial ratting and rabbiting sport up and down countryside ditches and hedgerows throughout Britain. So, although the majority of strains are today most likely to be show types, I thought the breed well worth including here. I was, however, somewhat amused by the reply to the question posed on an Internet forum asking, "where can I find a good Cairn of working strain?" – in answer to which, the following was posted: "the best place to look would be the nineteenth century"!

As a piece of interesting history, it would appear that the Cairn was much in favour as an otter-hunting dog. At the end of the Victorian period, one particular owner had a pack which killed 51 in two seasons (and, in addition, 32 foxes) and, in France, in the 1920s, a certain Mme de Parseval, who lived in the Oise department, had a pack of Cairns with which she regularly hunted otters.

Dandie Dinmont

Even though you'd be hard pressed to find a true working example of the breed in this day and age, I have included the Dandie Dinmont in this section purely because of its importance in the make-up of other established breeds – amongst which are, it is believed, the Bedlington and Sealyham. Originally a type which had been around the border counties since the early 1700s where it was used against badgers, fox and otter, it eventually bred true and was given its present moniker after a character in Sir Walter Scott's novel, *Guy Mannering*. Scott was personally fond of the breed and owned several; just a few of which went by the names of, "Mustard", "Pepper", "Catchup", "Ginger" and "Spice": he must have had a sense of humour (or respect for their origins) as before being given its current name, the breed was known as the "Mustard and Pepper Terrier" because of their colouring!
NB: *See more on the naming of hounds and terriers at the end of this chapter.*

Fox Terriers

Extremely popular in Britain in the past, working examples of both smooth-coated and wire-haired fox terriers (especially the wire-haired variety) are, for some reason, nowadays more often seen in my adopted country of France where they are used for work underground, particularly in connection with badger-digging which, provided that certain legalities are adhered to and complied with, is still legal.

Even as early as the 1920s, fox terriers were being exported abroad until, in 1931, Captain Lucas was moved to remark that "Probably no British breed of dog has ever won such universal popularity abroad as the fox-terrier."

Still, however, very much in evidence in Britain as hunt terriers in the early part of the twentieth century (possibly due to their ability to run with the hounds), their popularity began to wane in the period between the two World Wars, but not before some of their good qualities had begun to be bred into the modern-day Jack Russell.

Quite what the Parson Russell would have had to say about this is open to speculation as, from time to time, the fox terrier had been crossed with the bulldog or bull-terrier. Russell was known to have been against such cross-breeding due to the fact that, in his opinion, it made the resultant puppies too "hard". As he said (and it was further quoted by Lucas), "The difference between a fox terrier and a bull terrier is as follows: The fox terrier tackles his quarry for the love of sport and goes on undeterred by punishment. A bull terrier fights with blind ferocity in his desire to kill."

Fig 20: Both wire-haired and smooth-coated types of fox terrier are popular in France – where they are still used legally to dig out both fox and badger.

Jack Russell (or Parson Jack Russell)
Needing no introduction to anyone, the Jack Russell (in all its long/short legged, smooth/broken-coated guises) is possibly the best known and, arguably, most popular terrier of all time. It is, however, interesting to note that, until relatively recently, the Jack Russell was considered a type rather than a breed: Geoffrey Sparrow, writing in his book, *The Terrier's Vocation* (first published privately in 1949), made the following footnote: "Frequent references are made to the Jack Russell in here and elsewhere. By this I mean a white terrier, black or tan markings, a little up on the leg and with a good shoulder."

Whatever your personal thinking as regards type versus breed, it would be rare to find a ratting team or rabbit hunting bobbery pack that didn't include at least a couple of "Jacks" in its line-up!

Fig 21: Jack Russell terriers should be "a little up on the front with a good shoulder". Photo: Greg Knight (www.ruralshots.com)

Lakeland

The Lakeland continues to flourish as a working terrier. Some might say that it is more correct to refer to them far more generally as "Fell Terriers" as one could then include the Patterdale (red or black in colouring), and the rarely heard of Elterwater.

Arguably, the colouring of the Lakeland came about as a result of crosses with the old English Black and Tan (see also Manchester Terriers below) and Welsh terriers. It is also thought by some to have originally contained a certain amount of Bedlington blood in its make-up. Far more knowledgeable than I, "Lakeland" aficionados might well dispute this claim – but please don't shoot me; I am, in this instance, only the messenger!

On the back of that, the somewhat generic term, "Fell Terrier" can be somewhat confusing: the Fell and Moorland Working Terrier Club say that: '… unless bred as a type/family/line, [individuals] will often throw different types in the same litter" – which suggests to me, an amalgam of several types

Fig 22: A good-looking Fell terrier type. Photo: Greg Knight (www.ruralshots.com)

of terriers bred on the Lakeland farms (the owners and tenants of which were, in the main, enthusiastic killers of foxes due to the threat to their day-to-day livelihood) and mated with others purely because of an individual's working ability rather than any specific genetic lines being followed.

Manchester Terrier

From the industrial north, the Manchester is the result of a cross between the old Black and Tan Terrier – which was common throughout Britain during the mid-nineteenth century – and the whippet. The result was mainly used for ratting but, like the Bedlington, capable of both that and rabbiting. It seems that it might nowadays be virtually impossible to find a true working strain of Manchester terrier even though several were being worked as recently as the 1970s. However, one person who is keeping the working tradition alive is Martin Kirkbride of Pestforce (Oldham and District) who has a couple of very useful looking specimens that accompany him on his daily rounds! Interestingly, working Manchester terriers seem more common in the USA where those of the "standard" size (as opposed to the "toy") are seen to compete in earth dog trials.

Fig 23: Working Manchester terriers are rarely seen these days.

It's been suggested to me during the course of writing this book that, if anyone wanted to recreate a working Manchester type, breeding a Jagd terrier (they originate from Germany) with a black working whippet and then selectively breeding from the offspring might, although a long-term "project", eventually have a successful outcome.

Norfolk and Norwich
The only obvious difference between these two breeds is the fact that one has "pricked" ears (the Norwich) and the other does not. They are otherwise the same in colouring and equal in size and weight. When they first became known in the middle of the nineteenth century, as well as being used for entering to fox and badger underground, they were also very popular with Cambridge undergraduates who, it was said, used to smuggle them into their lodgings so that they could enjoy a bit of rat and rabbit hunting along the banks and surrounding countryside of the River Cam.

In *Hunt and Working Terriers* (1931), Jocelyn Lucas mentioned that the Norwich had the alternative name of the Trumpington terrier but that, no

Fig 24: A black and tan Norfolk stud dog typical of the mid 20th century. Photo: Mandy Shepherd

matter what they were called, they should only ever weigh around the 10lb (4.5kg) mark. He also commented on their possible modern origins and cited a certain Mr Nichols from Wymondham; Mr Low, a vet; J. E. Cooke, a past Master of the Norwich staghounds, and Mr R. J. Read, as being instrumental in the breeding and development of the Norwich terrier.

As to their working capabilities, it is definitely worth noting (bearing in mind the likely readership of this book) that, in 1929, Norwich terrier enthusiast, the Hon. Mrs. Richard Hoare, from London, "took her dogs up to Scotland, and they killed over forty rabbits on their own in ten weeks." As a testament to their drive and tenacity, Lucas also pointed out that the same lady commented on the fact that, "despite their small size ... they can run all day with horses."

Another sporting lady of the same era had a "pack" of four Norwich terriers which (again in Scotland) killed over 400 rabbits in a single season. She also said that her dogs were good ratters but that, where she was, "rats were scarce". Whether this was a natural phenomena or the result of her terriers' efforts is open to speculation!

Plummer Terriers
No book of this nature would be complete without mention of the Plummer Terrier – bred by David Brian Plummer, terrier and long-dog aficionado and prolific writer. Bred originally as a ratting dog, the breed is, according to the Plummer Terrier Club, "a composite of Jack Russell, Bull terrier, beagle and Fell terrier". Plummer initially started out with a small pack of rat hunting dogs, a strain of Jack Russell Terrier he originally called the Huddlesford Rat Pack and it was from these that the Plummer terrier was developed. In his book, *Omega*, (the story of his most famous Jack Russell bitch) Brian Plummer wrote: "I suppose I've always been keen to have a breed of dog called after me ... [when] I am hurriedly shuffled into a shabby grave because my mourners' ferrets are getting restless, perhaps these brown and white bull terrier-headed psychopaths I've set out to breed will be called Plummer Terriers."

Rest easy Brian, they are!

Scottish
Known for some years as the Aberdeen, the Scottish terrier was originally more like a black Cairn without any of the exaggerated muzzle which is seen in today's specimens. If a working strain can be found, it might well be worth including in the kennel of a rabbiting and ratting enthusiast. During research for this book, I did contact several terrier organisations in Scotland in the hope of finding out more. Sadly, and despite several follow-up emails, nothing was forthcoming – which is a huge shame as one would have thought that they would be keen to promote the breed!

So it is that we are left only with a few comments from the past. Lucas, for example, mentioned that, generally, "old Scottish keepers always used to keep a terrier or two of the Cairn or West Highland type". He furthermore suggested that a Scottish terrier was generic and the term might include any variety of terrier bred and used in the Highlands and Islands. Other opinions differ and it seems that the Scottish (sometimes spelt with only one "t") is, and always has been, a distinct breed.

Such proof might be gained from old records: King James VI of Scotland, apparently sent six "Scottish" terriers to France as a gift and, even earlier than that, John Lesley, Bishop of Ross, talked of similar dogs. Joshua Reynolds painted a portrait of a young girl with a dog looking remarkably like a Scottish terrier – as did Sir Edwin Landseer (famous for his painting "Monarch of the Glen"). In 1860 (some 60 years earlier than when Lucas suggested that it was a type rather than a breed), a dog show in Birmingham held a Scottish terrier class. Other records are of the opinion that the Scottish terrier was a descendent of the Skye – and describe a dog that was "rough-coated, short-legged" and was probably bred differently in various parts of Scotland, i.e. each strain of the breed was distinct to a particular area.

That they were tenacious there can be no doubt: in certain parts of the country, the "Scottie" was known as a "Diehard" – and was named as such because of the fact that George, the 4th Earl of Dumbarton, owned a pack of Scottish terriers that were so brave as to fear nothing. It was this pack that was supposed to have inspired the name of the Earl's army regiment: "The Royal Scots Dumbarton's Diehard".

Sealyham

The Sealyham might well make a worthwhile addition to a rabbiting and ratting pack. Like the Jack Russell, Plummer and Lucas terriers, the Sealyham owes its existence to a single individual, in this case, a certain Captain Edwards of Sealyham House, Wales. It was he who set about producing a "short-legged, hard-coated terrier with a strong jaw and a white body that would go anywhere and tackle anything" and, after his death in 1891, others took up the cause until in 1911, the Sealyham was being bred sufficiently "true" to be recognised by the Kennel Club. The Sealyham Club had, however been formed some three years earlier – and a year later (in 1912), the Sealyham Terrier Breeders and Badger Digging Association was formed. Its main aim was, according to Theo Marples writing in his book *The Sealyham Terrier* (1937), the "protecting and developing the working attributes of the dog so that it did not degenerate into a merely ornamental show dog".

While they might arguably be more difficult to find than the show varieties in this day and age, working strains still exist and the Working Sealyham Terrier Club (founded in 2008) is, as might be expected given its title, very proactive, both hunting and showing regularly in many parts of Britain. These include summer ratting trips along the riverbank, rabbiting and attending game fairs.

Two of the main enthusiasts of the working type are Harry Parsons (founder of the WSTC) and his partner Gail Westcott who have "worked tirelessly over the past few years to highlight the plight of the working Sealyham terrier. They own 10 Kennel Club registered dogs, which they

Fig 25: Working strains of Sealyhams might be hard to find but they still exist.

work as a hunting pack along with a few Jack Russells." (Quoted from a *Shooting Times* article published in 2013.)

<u>Sporting Lucas</u>
Jocelyn Lucas has been mentioned several times in this section. He was a very keen sportsman of the early twentieth century, particularly in connection with his pack of Sealyhams – which, unbelievably, were said to have accounted for some 3,000 rabbits annually. However, somewhat concerned that his strain was beginning to produce some heavy "cloddy" offspring, in the 1940s, he decided to outcross with the Norfolk terrier and, with some judicious matings, produced the Lucas terrier breed. The breed flourished for several decades but eventually began to lose some of the characteristics originally desired by Lucas and subsequent owners.

In the early 1990s, Brian Plummer (see the *Plummer Terrier* above) became involved with trying to reinstate some of these lost characteristics and used one of his terriers in order to eventually produce what is now known as the Sporting Lucas Terrier. The Sporting Lucas Terrier Association was set up in 2003; its aim being to provide information and keep owners in touch with one another.

Welsh

Not all that dissimilar in looks and stance to a typical Lakeland, the Welsh terrier is almost certainly descended from the rough coated black and tan terriers previously mentioned in this section. Like the fox terrier, it was originally expected to run alongside the huntsman (not with the actual hunting pack itself) of Welsh hounds and, when required, bolt foxes from the crags and slate of North Wales.

Even as far back as the late 1920s, it had been written that "the ordinary show Welsh terrier is … [likely] to be too big to be of any practical use" but, bearing in mind the fact that we are no longer looking for dogs that will go to ground, if a working strain could be found, the breed would certainly have stamina enough to be included in any planned rabbiting and ratting forays. A group of friends on the Welsh/English border have an unofficial pack of terriers and lurchers; amongst which are three generations of pure-bred, show-bred Welsh – thus proving that at least some examples of this breed are still "up for it" and have not lost their working qualities!

West Highland White

Thompson Gray in his *Dogs of Scotland* (1891) refers to a visit made by a Captain Mackie to Poltalloch for the purpose of seeing a white variety of terrier. The person he visited was another military man; a certain Colonel Malcolm of Poltalloch who, although he undoubtedly developed the West Highland White breed, nevertheless insisted that similar examples had been seen in Ross-shire, Skye, and many parts of Argyle for many years previous. They had to be strong, supple and resourceful and, unlike many terrier types, able to follow fox, otter and badger up and down craggy hillsides, and under, over and between rocks, rather than go to ground.

According to some records, the "Westie" was first called the "Poltalloch Terrier" and was, at one time, known as the "Scottish White". Although the breed is today seldom worked as Colonel Malcolm intended, there are, however, still some enthusiasts who rate the right sort as being good rabbiters and ratters; however, even decades ago, the breed was already being considered a little too soft for serious work as its tenacity and jaw power was a little suspect and, as Lucas remarked at the time, "they are chiefly known for show or as companions, for which purpose they are well suited, since they are very nice dogs, take up little room and require little exercise". Perhaps then, not exactly the obvious first choice for anyone thinking of adding to, or forming their own terrier pack!

Wheaten

Bred originally as an "all-round" dog for use amongst the Irish farming community, where it was used as a guard, rounder-up of livestock and for ratting around the buildings, I was, I must admit, in two minds as to whether or not to include the Wheaten terrier in this list but, as there are many sportsmen and women who might be reading this in Ireland, I thought that perhaps I should as it's one of their native breeds. From a working terrier Internet forum, it appears that "there are still quite a few wheatens" in the south that are performing well, although you will probably find it hard to get in touch with any wheaten men, unless you have a very good contact that could make an introduction. Other general comments include the opinions that the breed can be "aggressive", "not for the faint-hearted" and "not good with livestock or other dogs". There are, though, exceptions to every rule and I guess it is as much a question of bloodlines and breeding as it is general temperament.

Fig 26: A superb trio of working terriers ready for action. Photo: Greg Knight (www.ruralshots.com)

Two other terrier breeds from Ireland are the Kerry Blue and Glen of Imaal – a region south-east of Knockanarrigan in County Wicklow in Ireland.

Yorkshire
When one looks at the modern show-type Yorkshire terrier with its carefully groomed long silky coat and the traditional ribbon holding hair back from its eyes, it is easy to forget that, when it first originated, it was very much a sporting dog. Today, however, it is no longer classed in the "terrier" groups and is, instead, placed alongside the "toy" breeds. Nonetheless, I have on one memorable occasion, seen a little pack of four very spirited Yorkshire terrier types (sans flowing locks and ribbons!) owned by the wife of a gundog breeder friend, acquit themselves very well when dealing with an infestation of rats in a chicken-run. Killers they most definitely were. They also made ideal family pets within the home environment. Food for thought!

COLOURING AND COATS
As has already been noted in some of the above, many hounds and terriers have colouring distinctive to the breed. As a reminder, the Blue de Gascogne hounds are named after the region of France in which they originated – and also because of their blue "ticked" coats. Colour-wise, according to George Johnston, bi-coloured examples of the true Artesian Normand basset are "very seldom seen and are not encouraged". He also says that "the dominant colour is the full black blanketed tricolour with white extremities and a rich tan on the head, ears, shoulders and quarters". Occasionally a deer-red coloured hound occurs and, although undoubtedly attractive, are not popular amongst aficionados.

That the Dandie Dinmont was alternatively known as "mustard and pepper" terriers is a result of their colouring and, to be a true Plummer terrier, examples of that breed should, according to the standard laid out by the club, possess "a bright fiery red tan coat, accompanied by white on legs and collar".

Interestingly, for many years it was thought that any all-white whelps of some terrier breeds should be culled as white was considered wrong, weak, undesirable and even unlucky. Fortunately, the advantage of white terriers as being able to be seen at a distance eventually prevailed and many, such as the Malcolm family (who developed the West Highland White), the Duke of Argyle and other breeders of influence actively promoted them.

Above, Fig 27: Not all packs have a preference for hounds of a particular colour!
Below, Fig 28: Some terrier types can be broken-coated or smooth.. Photo: Robert Latham.

In beagle packs, whilst "a good horse is never a bad colour", it is quite obvious that there is a preference for certain markings, whether it be lemon and white or of the more traditional foxhound colour of black, tan and white. Beagles are nowadays almost always smooth-coated but in the past, wire-coated types have been described by the likes of writers such as Blaine in 1840, and Robert Leighton in 1912. As has been mentioned in the relevant section, the coats of some basset types can be wiry or rough-coated and it is possible that one of these, the Griffon Vendeen, was used to help create the old wire-coated beagle just described.

On the question of coats, it is widely felt that the rough-coated Borders, Fell terriers and broken-coated Jack Russell types have an advantage over silky, smooth-coated dogs when it comes to withstanding wet or cold conditions, and for pushing through brambles. On the negative side, however, it is possible to overlook any wounds. One experienced terrierman tells me that, in his opinion, it is the density of a coat rather than whether or not a dog is smooth or rough-haired which matters. "A dense jacket, whether rough or smooth, is the most ideal type. This will keep out much of the rain and wind. A soft, open coat is not particularly desirable; a soft silky one the worst of all."

SIZE MATTERS!

The size of hounds quite often depends on the type of country over which they hunt. An average height of a foxhound might be 25 inches (63cm), a harrier 20 inches (50cm) and a beagle around the 15 inches (38cm) mark but hounds which hunt over moorland and stone walls could well be a little taller than this and, conversely, hounds that hunt over flat grass or arable land and have never seen a ditch, wall or fence, other than perhaps a barbed-wire one, will be quite a bit smaller. To be eligible to show at the like of Peterborough, though, beagles must not exceed 16 inches (40cm) in height. Bassets vary according to the particular type but generally range between 13-15 inches (33-38cm). The Grand Basset Vendeen might, however, be a little taller than this and heavier-looking in stance and appearance.

The size of most terriers, because of the traditional nature of their work prior to the Hunting Act, was originally dictated by the need for them to be small enough to go to ground, yet strong enough to keep themselves out of trouble from whatever might be encountered whilst doing so.

There was, in many hunting establishments, a long-held theory that leggy, narrow terriers would be able to enter a small earth more readily than one that was half the height but was over-broad across the chest or behind the shoulder. Having said that, a reasonably broad chest is important as, together with a well-sprung rib-cage, it will ensure that there is plenty of room for the lungs and heart – hence the reason that, at terrier shows, the judge places great importance on the "spanning" of dogs under his scrutiny.

However, in compliance with the Hunting Act, it is far more likely that terriers will nowadays be used above ground and whilst the longer-legged types might have the advantage when actually engaged in a hunt, a smaller one can slip through the bottom growth of a thick hedgerow while a bigger one might be left struggling in the first bramble patch!

Fig 29: Originally, working terriers needed to be small enough to go to ground – yet strong enough to keep out of trouble. Photo: Greg Knight (www.ruralshots.com)

DESIRABLE ATTRIBUTES

Generally, the basic attributes necessary for any working hound or terrier are very similar. So too are their requirements when it comes to care, kennelling and health – of which more in the appropriate section of this book.

... In hounds

General conformation is important and hounds, whatever the breed, must possess speed, size and nose and, in general, an overall ability to hunt. If registered hounds happen to show well on the flags, that is certainly a desirable bonus, and whilst any dog can be persuaded to show itself by good handling the basic conformation has, nonetheless, to be there in the first place.

Whatever size the actual hounds may be (see Size Matters! above), the pack as a whole ought to be level if it is to have any chance of hunting

Fig 30: A well-balanced and good-looking pack of bassets. Photo: Greg Knight (www.ruralshots.com)

together without a leader running well in advance and the stragglers trailing along behind. If such a situation arises, probably the only thing for the masters and/or huntsman to do is to draft those hounds to another pack which has slower or faster hounds.

A good voice is very definitely a considerable attribute – not only does a hound giving tongue whilst on the scent sound absolutely amazing (The Greek writer Hippolyta declared: "I never heard so musical a discord, such sweet thunder") but its vocal range can help indicate so many things during the course of a hunt – from the hesitant "owning" of the line to being in full cry. Conversely, one wouldn't want a hound that "babbles" and gives false information both to you and its fellow pack members.

... In terriers

Terriers are very rarely silent, especially when close up to their quarry and an occasional yap might indicate the possible presence of a nearby rat whilst a team of them "screaming" with excitement can only mean that they are almost on top of their quarry. A terrier that gives tongue in cover is also a desirable asset and quite often you can tell when they're onto something just by the noise they make.

By its very nature, a terrier's potentially main problem is that of control. Obedience is key! This is generally obtained by training so a very desirable attribute is what one might term "biddability" – a quality most likely to be found as a result of an individual's genetic make-up and in-bred temperament.

In a pack of terriers, it is quite often noticed that one individual (quite often a female rather than as, one might naturally expect, a male animal) is the leader and so it is imperative that this one in particular is biddable and will easily respond to commands as it is from her that the other pack members will take their lead. As one experienced terrier handler put it, "even if they question the human element, they must never question their 'top dog' … if the canine pack leader is thoroughly trained, there will be few problems when it comes to the handler controlling the pack."

To the overall list of a terrier's desirable attributes can also be added, a good nose, a desire to find and a willingness to get on with the job. "Gameness" is a word often associated with terriers – by that is meant a willingness to work after rabbits and rats despite having to face dense bramble, hillside gorse or, perhaps worst of all as far as their pads are concerned, beds of nettles. More particularly, it can be applied to a dog that will continue catching and worrying rats despite having suffered several bites. Conversely, a terrier lacking gameness will chase rats but often doesn't possess the courage to catch and kill them – or if they do pick one up, will drop it almost immediately for fear of being bitten. Unless it is born of youth and inexperience, such behaviour can very definitely be considered an undesirable fault.

Fig 31: A team of working terriers of the right sort!. Photo: Greg Knight (www.ruralshots.com)

UNDESIRABLE FAULTS

Following on from the above, it is also well worth mentioning – albeit briefly – a few negative points sometimes found in working hounds and/or terriers. As a rule, most hound breeds are a pretty placid lot and can be kept kennelled together without much disagreement other than the occasional reminder of who is "top dog". Sadly, the same cannot always be said of terriers.

Temperament is everything and some breeds of terrier can be kept in the same kennel without mishap – one does, however, only need one rogue individual to upset the apple cart! One particular owner remarked, "if the temperament is wrong, you shouldn't give it house room." The same person was also of the opinion that some people tend to mate different types of terrier in the hope of achieving the ultimate and perfect dog but that, quite often, doing so can have the opposite effect and may only actually succeed in producing "aggressive and dangerously game terriers … with a ruinous effect on the packing instinct".

To withstand the rigours of a day's hunting, all need to possess stamina and drive. Drive should not, however, be confused with physical speed as, if speed is bred into a dog (particularly a hunting hound) beyond a certain point, other attributes are bound to suffer; after all, a dog is only as good as its nose and there can be no advantage in breeding fast limbs which might cause an animal to overrun the scent of its quarry. A lack of stamina is very often responsible for the development of "skirting". Without stamina certain hounds and terriers soon begin to look for ways and means of cutting corners and anticipating the movements of the intended quarry and of the more reliable members of the pack. Avoiding all that is, of course, a result of careful breeding but there is one particular requirement which has not necessarily to do with anything in the bloodline: the need for a steadiness to livestock.

Sometimes a propensity to riot on wildlife such as deer; or too keen an interest in sheep or chickens can be in the young animal's genes but it is also possible that it is simply a matter of youthful curiosity and exuberance. While it is perhaps easier said than done, any potential problems must be nipped in the bud as soon as practicable as it is too much of a responsibility to take an untrustworthy dog out hunting. In times past, hunts that had a particular problem with a hound (or more) that proved impossible to stop after deer or sheep would euthanize an individual rather than risk it causing damage, or draft it to a pack somewhere where such distractions were unlikely to be encountered.

Fig 32: Stamina and drive are definitely desirable qualities!. Photo: Darren Clark)

Wilfulness is not generally to be encouraged but it seems that there are occasions when it can be tolerated – especially by fans of the various basset breeds! One remarked that "they're out to please themselves, not their owners", whilst Peter Brook, owner of *Baily's Hunting Directory* (a fantastic source of information on the various packs throughout the UK) mentioned in a *Country Life* interview that, "They're enormously wilful, but they have so much character and are so much fun that you forgive their peccadilloes."

PEDIGREE, PURE, OR POOCH?
Some hounds and terriers registered with the Kennel Club have proven pedigrees that carry little or no weight with the various associations concerned with official hunting. Some working hounds registered with the likes of the MFA, AMBH and MBHA have pedigrees going back generations and yet they are of a type that carries no weight with the Kennel Club! The whole business is a veritable minefield – especially when one adds into the mix the fact that some terrier breeds are recognised by the Kennel Club whilst others, despite the care with which dedicated owners and enthusiasts have bred true to form for many decades, are not. Basically, the difference

between a pedigree and purebred animal can be defined as per the answer below which appears on *Yahoo!*:

> "A pedigree is a listing of ancestors on both the sire's and dam's side, going back some number of generations. The function of a registry [such as that provided by the Kennel Club], is to keep these records, and certify to their accuracy. So if you have a puppy born to registered parents, when the puppy is registered, the registry will look in their records and provide a certified copy of its pedigree."

If all of a pup's ancestors are of the same breed, you have a purebred dog. If they are of different breeds then, at the risk of stating the obvious, you have a mixed breed and the Kennel Club could not register such an animal. However, a person could create their own record of "pedigree" regardless of the different breeds that were involved and this might prove quite useful if they were trying to establish a new breed or type and wished to establish their own registry in order to keep track of the ancestors and offspring of various matings.

Hoping to further clarify rather than confuse, to summarize, it might also be said that non-pedigree dogs could either be purebreds without papers, or crossbreeds. Pedigree dogs have up to five generations of family history recorded and are completely purebred – and are registered with the Kennel Club. If you buy a purebred without Kennel Club pedigree papers then technically it is not purebred as you have none of the dog's ancestry recorded to prove it!

Packs of hounds might well include Kennel Club registered dogs as well. Mrs Daphne Thorne mentions this when talking of how the Barony Bassets were formed. "The original hounds came in 2006 from David Vaughan, who had a very good little pack in Shropshire. He gave me two couple of hounds which were steady and sensible and I am eternally grateful to him for this. Nick Valentine gave me two whelps of his own breeding, and has given me several more since then, whelps and entered hounds. I purchased a Kennel Club registered dog hoping to use him on my bitches, but although he finds, hunts and kills with great vigour and voice, I have decided not to breed from him as he has never learned to pace himself and consequently gets tired before the end of the day. Another KC registered dog hunts with us and is better able to pace himself and stay the whole day. He was second at Peterborough a couple of days ago [2013] and has also been placed at Crufts."

Fig 33: Litter of pure-bred, pedigree Border puppies.

One other thing might also benefit from some clarification under this particular sub-heading and that is the fact that when a master of hounds mentions that theirs is a "mixed pack", they are not referring to a pack of mongrels, but more that it is made up of both dogs and bitches.

THE MAKE-UP OF A BOBBERY PACK
The renowned huntsman, Captain Ronnie Wallace began his hunting career as a nine year-old with a bobbery pack of small beagles, terriers and a golden retriever. Almost all breeds of dogs have been known to take to rabbit and rat hunting; nonetheless, some make better rabbiters and ratters than others, just as one individual dog may take to the game more readily than another even when out of the same litter. So, if you want to enjoy as much sport as possible, you must choose members of your "pack" with care and forethought.

As we have seen, some of the unofficial, unregistered packs of hounds and terriers organised by friends and acquaintances who are out for sport and to provide a service for farmers and landowners by eradicating some of their rabbits and rats, are made up of all manner of individual canines and while these will, in the main, be beagles, bassets and terriers of various types, there may also be found a few dogs of undetermined parentage!

They are likely to include lurchers – and whilst I mentioned at the outset, that "sighthounds" were the subject of books other than this – it has to be said that one could do far worse than incorporate a lurcher-type into the day's sport as their intelligence, tenacity, running and killing capabilities are a wonderful asset.

Some enthusiastic "pack" owners have also deliberately out-crossed from a particular pure-bred animal in order to achieve all the desirable attributes (and hopefully, none of the undesirable faults!) that may be found in other breeds. It would not, for instance, be unusual to see a bobbery pack member containing the bloodlines of a beagle for "nose" and scenting ability, a terrier for tenacity and controlled "aggression", and a spaniel (often a cocker) for "drive".

There might also be some individual pack members which have bull terrier in their genes. Their inclusion in the make-up of some sporting dogs is no new thing and breeders of the eighteenth century introduced bulldog blood into coursing greyhounds in order to add a bit of their "hardness". Over the ensuing years, bull terriers were mated with Sealyham types and Brian Plummer did something similar when he became involved with creating the Sporting Lucas terrier.

Fig 34: A typical "bobbery" pack is likely to include hounds, terriers and maybe the odd running dog. Photo: Greg Knight (www.ruralshots.com)

Fig 35: One cannot fail but to have good sport with a hound/terrier combination!

Some of the possible reasons why bull terrier crosses might have been made were explained in an excellent article by John Glover in *The Countryman's Weekly*: "Rabbiting in harsh conditions … can tax a dog's reserves whilst ratting on big numbers also depletes energy, even in tried and tested game terriers such as Patterdale/Fell types. When big numbers of rats are killed during a day's hunting a bigger, stronger dog may be better equipped to cope with the constant lift and shake that can cause fatigue in conventional terriers … In saying this I definitely don't intend to knock or take anything away from the gallant tried and tested types, but am instead suggesting that a half bred Bull or Bull blooded, larger terrier may have better stamina."

A bobbery pack consisting of different breeds can have certain advantages over those containing just hounds or terriers. A basset or dachshund in amongst a group of terriers, for example, is better able to own a "cold" scent than are most terriers and, whilst terriers, on having lost "their" rabbit will go searching for another, a hound or dachshund will persevere on the line of the hunted one. A huntsman of a bobbery pack did, though, once state that such tenacity can have its drawbacks: "Sometimes the terriers were busy chivvying a fresh rabbit while old Mayo [a basset] was still booming away on the line of another which had been killed twenty minutes before!"

NAMING HOUNDS AND TERRIERS

"Mayo" (see immediately above) might well be a good name for a basset but more frequently hounds are blessed with somewhat more traditional monikers. Examples might include illusions of grandeur such as Viscount and Countess – and a whole host of others based on ancient writings such as Halcyon and Actaeon. Actually, on reflection, the latter is, perhaps, not the best name to give a hound as, in Greek mythology, Actaeon was a huntsman dismembered by members of his own pack!

Changing times surely mean that some imaginative Masters must now be giving puppies more modern names – it would be good to think that, somewhere out in kennels, there lives at least one Freeserve, Twitter or Google. Perhaps there are: Jeremy Whaley, Master of the South Downs Bloodhounds tells me that he will always consider anything for the name of a hound and was, when I asked him, apparently "thinking of having an Ipad or Ipod in the litter I have in kennels now".

Quite often hounds are given the names of professions and it is common to hear a huntsman call out for Fireman or Barrister. Place names are another option and many a master has resorted to a map book or atlas! Whatever, the traditional naming of hounds is a fascinating subject; so much so that a number of the old hunting books have a chapter, or at least several pages devoted to the problem. Peter Beckford, writing in his 1810 book, *Thoughts on Fox and Hare Hunting*, opined that, "Pipers and Fiddlers for sake of their music, we will not object to; but Tipplers and Tapsters your kennels will be much better without." Sir Rowland, 4th Baronet of Nostell (in West Yorkshire) kept a pack of fox hounds and his stud-book can still be seen today – his choice of Aimwell or Dauntless would be good names for a dog to live up to, but Arsenic, Noxious, or Trollop?

There was, and possibly still is, in existence, an 1814 portrait of the long defunct Raby hounds painted by H.B. Chalon which named his canine sitters as being, Craftsman, Benedict, Merryman, Baronet, Mahomet, Modish, Symphony, Maynard, and Governess. Also in the picture was Jasper; a terrier who, according to Charles Richardson, a foxhunting writer who described the painting almost a century later, was apparently, "a dark-coloured, smooth-coated, prick-eared, and very verminty dog, whose breed it would be difficult to name these days".

Fig 36: Hounds are usually given very traditional names.

Terrier titles

Northern terriers, no matter what breed, have generally been given short, sharp, no nonsense names such as Grip, Rock or Tyke. Despite that, one of the Fell packs (the Melbreak, I think), had, at the time I used to hunt with them regularly, a wiry nondescript terrier called Spider and, once you'd seen her scrambling up rocks with her long legs out-splayed as if on suction pads, it was easy to see that no dog could ever have been more aptly-named. In the south, it seems things are different: Sarah Taylor, secretary to the Fell and Moorland Working Terrier Club, lives on Exmoor and says that "short names are more noticed anywhere from the Midlands up … down here, we generally choose longer ones such as Teazle and Nettle … and a terrierman nearby has three Patterdales called Chocolate, Biscuit and Brown, named purely because of their colour." When I spoke to her, Sarah herself had a Border terrier which answered to Gizmo!

Some owners, though, apparently, have no such imagination: Sir Walter Scott, whose fondness for Dandie Dinmont terriers we mentioned earlier

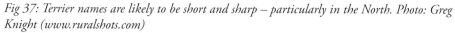

Fig 37: Terrier names are likely to be short and sharp – particularly in the North. Photo: Greg Knight (www.ruralshots.com)

in this chapter; noted the time when a Scottish farmer told an English visitor that, "I have six terriers at hame … there's Auld Pepper, and Auld Mustard, and Young Pepper and Young Mustard and Little Pepper and Little Mustard." Then, there is the well-known story relating to the late Sir Newton Ryecroft; one time master of the New Forest Hounds, who, when complimented for naming a hound after his daughter, replied, "Actually, I named it after a terrier I had … as I did my daughter."

Puppy christenings
It used to be a regular occurrence that a litter of puppies born to a Northern hunting establishment participated in a christening ceremony where drink (often a mixture of local ale and whisky) was poured into rather ornate silver or glass punchbowls and the pups were either anointed or completely dunked. Custom then dictated that members of the hunt would then be invited to partake of the contents of the bowl. Slightly more sanitised in this day and age, such traditions still continue on the edge of the Pennines but whether the title and chorus of Victorian hunting enthusiast, George Whyte-Melville's well-known song is referring to a puppy christening is open to doubt. Nevertheless, it encompasses a certain sentiment when it declares; Then drink, puppy drink,/And let every puppy drink/That is old enough to lap and to swallow,/For he'll grow into a hound/So we'll pass the bottle round,/And merrily we'll whoop and we'll holloa.

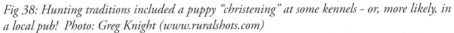

Fig 38: Hunting traditions included a puppy "christening" at some kennels - or, more likely, in a local pub! Photo: Greg Knight (www.ruralshots.com)

HUNTING WITH OTHERS

AS THE WEBSITE of a particular beagle pack says, "When the government banned hunting, they probably calculated that we would just give up and fade away. Well we haven't and hunting is now more popular than it ever has been. How have we prospered? The answer is trail-hunting." With this in mind, it probably makes logical sense to talk first about what happens at a traditional meet of hounds before then discussing how best to get involved and experience what some of the more informal bobbery packs have to offer. If you've never been out hunting before, making initial contact in order to find out about meet venues can sometimes be quite difficult as, perhaps understandably, those responsible for running a day might be wary of an unsolicited approach from a stranger.

As to whether you can take your own dog with you, it obviously depends on the type of hunting you are wishing to follow. While an informal ratting pack might encourage you to take your terrier and actively participate in the proceedings; the masters of an "official" pack may well have a policy of not allowing followers to take their animals along for fear of getting in the way, causing problems or distracting the pack. Others

Fig 39: Any followers with dogs should keep them well away from the pack at all times … but particularly at the Meet.

might stipulate that, as in this extract from a meet card, "People who bring their dogs to meets are requested to keep them well away from the hounds and if you then follow the hunt you must ensure your dog stays on a lead at all times to prevent him running after the pack and/or causing trouble within the pack or farm stock."

HUNTING SEASONS

As far as sport with the rabbit hunting packs are concerned (and the same applies equally to those who hunt an artificial trail), the season "proper" begins in October and ends in March. However, what is known as "Autumn Hunting" (or quite possibly, "Training Days") by the general hunting fraternity might take place a month earlier – depending on, where applicable, when the harvest allows. Any such meets are usually held early in the morning before the temperature rises and evaporates the scent and are traditionally part of the process of entering young hounds to hunting (see more in Sport with Your Dog). In Ireland, the beagle packs have to adhere to a strict season which, according to an article by Rachel Green in a past issue of *The Countryman's Weekly*, runs "from September 26 to February 28, by licence which is issued by the Department of Agriculture". (As an interesting aside, in the same article Rachel also mentions that "Here we find the real hound enthusiasts! They are a hardy bunch and have some great hunting.")

Fig 40: Hunting rats with terriers has no real season and is carried out both winter and summer. Photo: Greg Knight (www.ruralshots.com)

Hunting rats with terriers has, however, no real "season" as rats are such an ongoing problem and generally speaking, the more that can be killed no matter what the time of year, so much the better. Some, such as Harry Parson's pack of working Sealyhams, even hunt the riverbanks for rats in summer in much the same manner as the old packs of otterhounds – and what better way can there be to while away a few hours in the sunshine?

WHO GOES HUNTING?

Depending on the type of hunting, there is a huge range of enthusiastic followers ranging from teenagers to those well past retiring age. Supporting the traditional packs of hounds that have, since the Hunting Act, turned their hunting of hares to that of an artificial trail, might then, include a whole variety of people who enjoy a few hours in the British countryside and the opportunity to watch hounds work. Others, perhaps those involved with small ratting packs, are more "hands-on" and not only add their terriers to the pack, but are also prepared to shift a barn full of farming material if it is felt necessary for the efficiency of their dogs working! Nick Ridley, following Harry Parson's pack (see above), was "surprised at the kind of people who had made an effort to come along. I've been on a few terrier rat

Fig 41: All manner of people turn up to watch hounds – especially at the traditional Boxing Day Meet.

hunts and ... it can all be a bit macho ... [here] the 'followers' comprised families with children."

An article in the *Observer* written in October 2011, attempted to identify some of the reasons why many people hunt – and recorded comments from a couple of enthusiastic followers: "When I'm out in the field," said one, "I always get a great sense of privilege at the beauty, and the access to some lovely parts of England." Another mentioned the cameraderie, "What I love about the rural community is that it's a well-glued society of mutually supportive people. In the countryside there's another way of life." Conversely, a third pointed out the negative side by saying, "Once the winter proper comes you can be out in the field, freezing cold, utterly exhausted and wondering, 'Why am I doing this?'" Nonetheless, the fact remains that many of us will put up with more than a little discomfort simply to be a part of a wonderful experience.

MAKING CONTACT

Necessary information (telephone, email address et al) regarding the registered packs of hounds might be found on the *Baily's Hunting Directory* website or, alternatively, on search engine details pertaining to the various associations responsible for the well-being and good conduct of the many hound packs which hunt throughout Britain. For other private packs and those run legally, efficiently, but unofficially by a group of enthusiastic hound and terrier owners, making contact with them will prove more difficult as, unless directly involved, even the locals might not know of their existence. If, however, you are of a tenacious nature, nothing is impossible and a bit of detective work amongst the area's farmers and gamekeepers should eventually produce some results.

When you do eventually make contact, be prepared for the possibility of having to answer a few questions about yourself and your interest ... and maybe offer to supply a reference that will verify the fact that you are a legitimate would-be follower rather than an animal rights supporter (not that you cannot be both, of course!)

Although many registered hunts are contactable directly through their websites and/or emails, it should always be remembered that their secretaries are volunteers and may take time to answer any queries due to pressures of work and family commitments. Where telephone numbers are given (but no times between which to call), it always pays to be considerate and not ring at inappropriate moments such as likely meal times, on a Sunday, or in the late evening – in fact, think of when you get most annoyed about cold-calling from double-glazing sales personnel and the like and avoid doing the same! Should you choose to make contact with a letter, always ensure that you enclose a self addressed, stamped envelope for your reply as postage can prove quite costly and is money the hunt could better spend elsewhere.

It's also worth noting that towards the end of October/beginning of November each year, the Countryside Alliance promote Hunting Newcomers Week as part of it's campaign for hunting and it may be possible to gain a few introductions through this. As the name suggests, the Newcomers Week is intended mainly for those who want to experience a day's sport for the first time and all newcomers who attend a day's hunting are guided by an experienced hunt follower who explains everything that is going on. Contacting the Countryside Alliance in order to find out more could, therefore, prove quite worthwhile.

Fig 42: Contact the CA for details of their Hunting Newcomers" Week (Countryside Alliance).

A note for club secretaries

Every enquiry deserves an answer. Even though most secretary and similar positions are of an honorary nature and has to be fitted into whatever spare time is available, there is no point in agreeing to take on the job if you are not prepared to do all that is necessary for the smooth-running of the club or group. The job entails "public relations" and it is therefore important that any communication from anyone making contact for whatever reason, should be answered – and answered as promptly as possible.

A note or email acknowledging receipt is all that is necessary straight away. You may, for instance, want time to check on someone's credentials before answering a specific question (in which case, ask the enquirer to provide a "reference" or mutual contact you know and trust – see above).

WHERE IS THE MEET HELD AND WHEN?

Although it might be traditional for almost every pack in the country to be out on a Saturday and again at least once mid-week, there have been a few changes made since the Hunting Act, especially when it comes to following private packs of rabbit hounds. For instance, the Barony Bassets frequently hunt on a Sunday – as their website says, "… we all hunt with other packs on Saturdays and work during the week." It then goes on to state that meets are usually fixed "at the Master's convenience, once or twice weekly." Nick Valentine of the Ryeford Chase also appears to be flexible with regards to hunting days and is quoted as remarking, "We go … on any day to suit ourselves … and though we try to hunt on a Monday and Friday, if it's tipping with rain on Monday then we'll go on Tuesday instead."

When run on time-honoured lines, most packs stipulate the time, date and place of their meets on a printed "Meet Card" made available to all members and/or subscribers. These cards usually include information which takes in the whole of the season although some will only show the details up until, say Christmas, after which another card is printed to cover the remainder of the season.

Whereas foxhunting-type packs almost always meet at 11.00am, beagle and bassets generally meet in the early afternoon (many around 12.30). There is, though, one area of the British Isles where you might find rare exceptions to this rule, and that is in the "mill" valleys of West Yorkshire. Unlike most packs, the likes of the Colne Valley and Holme Valley customarily, on a Saturday, met at 10.30am, stopped for lunch a couple of hours or so later and then, at 1.30 or 2.00 in the afternoon, began again (sometimes even from a different location). At their mid-week meets, however, there was, generally, just a single afternoon turnout. The reason behind this unique Pennine habit is that this split hunting was originally created in order to take account of the fact that, whilst the gentry (who didn't have to toil to make a living) could enjoy their sport all day, the local mill workers – always an enthusiastic bunch when it came to following hounds in days gone by – could join the hunt after their morning shift.

Where a particular pack meet can vary, it might be outside a village pub, at a cross-roads or well-known landmark, in a farmyard or at the house of a supporter of the hunt – in which case it is often known as a "lawn meet" and is likely to be accompanied by a drop of port or similar and a sausage roll or two before the hounds move off.

Fig 43: Bassets moving off from the Meet. Photo: Greg Knight (www.ruralshots.com)

AT THE MEET

Apart from the fact that there are few more enjoyable sights than a pack of hounds being unvanned and that the late arrivals will miss this opening scenario, the newcomer will find it worth his while arriving at the scene of the meet at least quarter of an hour before the advertised time in order to make the acquaintance of other followers. If a complete tyro, say that you're out to see some sport but haven't the faintest idea of how to see it, where to go or what to look out for, there will be no shortage of helpful advice.

It is not all about hound work though. There is a very strong social side, and for some followers, a day's rabbiting or trail-hunting is as much an opportunity to mingle with like-minded friends. They will always manage to find something new to talk about, whether political or social, international or local. The meet often provides a focal point for other interests: for instance the amateur historian is bound to be interested in the fact that the green lane over which he is walking was once a minor Roman road. And, as well as affording the opportunity to learn a lot more about the immediate locality and countryside, following hounds gives access to ground on which one would otherwise be classed as a trespasser.

Whilst regular hunt members are encouraged to contribute to the hunt coffers via an annual subscription, casual visitors (that means you!) may be expected to pay for their enjoyment by means of the "cap". Almost literally, a question of handing the hat round (although in most cases nowadays, a draw-string cloth bag) the "cap" is collected by the hunt secretary or other member of the hunt. Therefore, you should always have some cash (between £5-10.00 would normally suffice) somewhere about your person. A few packs nowadays issue identity cards and is their way of overcoming any possible litigious claims, and also shows that all those who follow have been made aware of health and safety procedures and various risk assessments that may have been put in place.

Some dos and don'ts
In an effort to avoid the risk of falling foul of hunt staff, keep downwind of the pack and never walk in front of hounds as, by doing so, one runs the risk of foiling the scent and spoiling not only your sport but so too, that of others. Also, it is as well to remember the advice given by the Association of Masters of Harriers and Beagles who, in their *Introduction to Beagling*, say that, "No hunt of any kind could possibly function without the kindness, generosity and cooperation of farmers, landowners and 'keepers, who permit hounds to hunt across their land at no cost."

Whilst on the subject of etiquette and general good manners, it is perhaps worth noting the observations of the 10th Duke of Beaufort who was emphatic that no follower should be late to the meet, saying that "I find it a great nuisance having latecomers arriving from all sides, and I also think unpunctuality is extremely bad manners. 'Punctuality is the politeness of Princes' is by no means an idle saying …"

Another point to bear in mind (and more out of interest than for any other reason) is the somewhat archaic habit whereby followers of hounds have always traditionally greeted the master at the meet with a polite "Good morning, Master" – even if, as might well be the case with beagles and bassets, it is beyond noon when the meet takes place – and, at all other times, follower and master are on first name terms. Also, traditionally, when an individual left the field in order to return home, it was always customary that, wherever convenient, one sought out this particular hunt official and bade him "Good night, Master" – even if it was but early afternoon.

Fig 44: Beagles "un-vanning".

Whether you try and keep up with hounds (without getting in the way) or just find a vantage point from where you can watch them do their work is entirely up to you! As an article in *The Telegraph* once advised its readers; "Frustrated Steve Crams are welcome to try keeping up with the huntsmen, but shouldn't flinch at the prospect of 15 miles and a couple of river crossings. Most follow at a more sedate pace, or park themselves on a hilltop with a hip flask, stuffing bags and pockets with sloes whenever there is a lull."

HOW MANY HOUNDS?

How long is a piece of string? Typically, some registered packs might take out anywhere between 10 and 20 couple of hounds (hounds are always counted in "couples" i.e. two hounds equals one couple. An odd number, say nineteen, would be referred to as "nine and a half couple") whereas small packs might bring to the meet all but the elderly, infirm and in season! This brings us to the ins and outs of owning a large pack. The advantages are many, of course – more dogs, more options, more chances to hunt. After all, it's a rare day when the entire pack is down from illness or injury (except perhaps in the case of kennel cough ... of which more in Kennels; Health and Hygiene). There are always a percentage that won't be able to hunt on a given day, but that leaves the rest of the pack to choose from. Pack dynamics are such that there are leaders and there are followers, but there are times when the pack leaders aren't up to it and so the followers suddenly step up and take over. Hounds develop their skills over time and with experience, and in a pack the level of ability ebbs and flows with the age and experience of the dogs.

Nick Valentine frequently hunts with a pack of twenty-five couple of Petit Griffon Vendeens, however, Daphne Thorne says that she feels happiest when hunting a pack of between six and nine couple and further remarks that, "Their cry is so good that they sound just like fifteen couple of your average foxhounds!"

Some types of bassets, because of their natural passion and desire to hunt, are quite tenacious and, even by those who breed them, understand them and hunt them, are said to be a little "unruly" on occasions! For that

Fig 45: Hounds are always counted in "couples". Photo: Greg Knight (www.ruralshots.com)

reason, at least one person reckons that their "independent nature … makes them difficult to control in large packs" and maintains that "they are best worked as a single, brace or in small packs". Another says that they have a reputation for being "riotous and volatile … [will] hunt anything that moves … [and] will do everything in double-quick time …" More is, therefore, not necessarily better and Sir John Buchanan-Jardine, who hunted with just about every type of hound, said that the best hunts he ever had were with a small pack of four or five couple.

How many terriers?

As far as the number of terriers to be used for rabbiting are concerned, Colin Haynes, writing on the subject back in 1987, was of the opinion that, "Three terriers are about right for working thick hedges and a half dozen for small woods and spinneys." Further, Jack Ivester Lloyd had this to say on the matter: "I always enjoy the sight of two working together, especially if they are in the habit of doing so and have therefore developed a 'team spirit'. Indeed, while a single dog may be excellent for putting rabbits out to a gun, or for working in conjunction with a ferret, for hedgerow hunting at least two are necessary."

Fig 46: A couple of terriers which regularly work together will soon develop "team spirit"! Photo: Greg Knight (www.ruralshots.com)

HUNT STAFF

Those interested in knowing more about a day's hunting run along traditional lines might wish to find out a little of the "duties" of huntsman, masters, whippers-in and "quarry" so a few words included here might not come amiss.

The huntsman

Although it is often said that the way to a man's heart is through his stomach, the same cannot necessarily be said of hounds as, once they have learned to trust their huntsman, their loyalties will be to him and not the person who feeds them. Of course, in many circumstances it may be one and the same but primarily, the huntsman's duties are to make sure that his hounds work well together as a pack. To do so, he might need to encourage the tail hounds and steady the leading ones and, in the case of a check, make the decision as to whether or not to help hounds to recover the line by use of a cast.

Such technicalities need to be decided upon quickly and any other hunt staff and the field must abide by them otherwise the day's sport is doomed to failure. He is, then, arguably, the most important part of any hunting foray and there is some truth behind the assertion made by a very young Ronnie Wallace many years ago. Captain Wallace was one of the most famous huntsmen of the twentieth century and started his illustrious career at the age of nine with his own bobbery pack of a few beagles and terriers. Apparently he made himself huntsman and his brother Master, deeming the latter role by far the inferior one!

Masters of hounds

Although he hunted hounds, Wallace was also master of several packs in his time. In certain circles, he was known simply as "God" and he ruled his field with a rod of iron. In fact, as his obituary in *The Telegraph* recorded in 2002, "it was not unknown for members of the field, fearful of the rough side of his tongue, to hide rather than be discovered in the wrong place at the wrong time."

Generally, though, the role of a master is not to create fear amongst the followers (although there can be no doubt that it would help at times!), but more to oversee the management and conduct of the hunt both when out and in kennels. At one time, he or she would also have financed the whole kit and caboodle but it is nowadays more common for a hunt to be committee-run and, hopefully, self-financing. Technically, a master of hounds is responsible for deciding when and where hounds meet, in what direction a trail is to be laid or, in the case of a rabbit hunting pack, what cover is to be drawn. One of a master's most important duties is in the liaison between the hunt and landowners or farming tenants over whose ground hounds are hoping to hunt and in this task, he is often assisted by the huntsman in order that they both not only have excellent relations but also an excellent knowledge of the land over which they hunt.

Whippers-in

Whippers-in (never "whipper-ins"!) assist the huntsman in hound control, at times turning them back to him when a situation is not exactly as it should be. They are also often posted at some distance in the direction of where hunting is due to take place so as to keep an eye on things and possibly prevent hounds from crossing a road or changing from the scent onto something forbidden as a result of the Hunting Act. Almost always amateurs, whippers-in are enthusiastic and important members of the hunt and often help out in kennels at weekends and evenings. From personal experience, I would say that whipping-in is definitely the best way to learn more about hunting and how hounds work.

The "Quarry" and trail-layers

Such persons have probably never before been mentioned in a hunting book and are, with the exception of bloodhound packs which have always hunted the "clean boot", only necessary nowadays because of the current legislation brought about as a result of the 2004 Hunting Act.

Basically, their duties are pretty self-explanatory and, in the case of bloodhounds, the quarry must be quite fit and also, ideally know enough about how hounds work so as to be able to include a few tricks that might temporarily throw the pack off their scent in order to make the hunting more interesting. A bloodhound quarry will most likely set off three-quarters of an hour or so before hounds are laid on the line (a day's hunting might typically include three to six lines and cover anywhere between 10-20 miles in total) and there are half hour gaps between lines so that a further trail can be run.

Laying an artificial scent for other types of hunting packs involves dragging a scent impregnated bundle of rag or sack along the ground perhaps 20 minutes or so before hounds move off from the meet. This can be done from a horse, a bike or on foot, but the Masters of Foxhounds Association suggest that "good results may be best achieved using a combination of all three". Whatever method is used, the trail-layers should bear in mind the fact that it ought to be laid in such a way that it simulates a natural route that would be taken by a wild animal such as a fox or hare as it attempts to evade its pursuers. The MFHA also suggest that the trail should occasionally be lifted "for a distance of, say, 400 yards and then dropped again thus allowing the hounds to cast ... for the scent as they would ... when hunting a live quarry." They also make the very valid point that the less the huntsman or field know of the route of the trail, "the more the hunting will mimic its realistic and challenging form."

One trail-hunting pack's website describes the laying of a trail thus: "Before we meet ... one of the whips attaches a lure soaked with a smelly concoction that attracts the hounds to a piece of rope. He runs with this over the fields and through the woods making a trail. To add interest only the whip knows where the trail has been laid."

Fig 47: Laying a trail. Photo: Greg Knight (www.ruralshots.com)

ON THE TRAIL
Much mystery surrounds what the scent of an artificial trail might consist of and, as has been mentioned elsewhere, many permutations have been tried with varying degrees of success. Having talked to several masters and huntsmen, it seems that some hounds will not follow an artificial trail at all well unless it is in some way animal-based. The website of *HuntingAct.org* mentions that, "in the case of traditional fox hunting packs fox urine is often claimed to be used. The reason given for the use of animal-based scents is that if the Hunting Act is repealed the hounds do not have to be re-trained to hunt the natural quarry scent".

NB: See also Entering hounds to an artificial line in Sport with Your Hounds and Terriers.

THE SITUATION OVERSEAS

As has been shown in the Introduction, it is not just England and Wales that have complicated and sometimes bizarre legislation when it comes to hunting with hounds and terriers; it happens in other countries too! It is, for example, perfectly legal to hunt rabbits and hares in France (and even dig for badgers with terriers), but you would be breaking the law if you attempted coursing with lurchers, or any other form of sighthound. In Spain you can course hares and rabbits with any amount of dogs but in neighbouring Portugal, such sport is only allowed with two. In Germany, hunting with packs of hounds was banned as long ago as 1934 on the orders of Hermann Göring but, like France, it is still possible to organise digs with terriers.

Fig 48: In some countries, foxhunting continues in the time-honoured way…

Fig 49: … and in France and elsewhere, packs of terriers are used to hunt both fox and badger.

Australia

Hunting with sighthounds is illegal in Australia and, as far as other forms of hound and terrier work is concerned, the laws there are just as, if not more so, confusing than those imposed in the UK by the 2004 Hunting Act. Beagles were, though, imported into Australia with the direct intention of using them in the war against the ever-increasing rabbit population. In 1914, author Robert Kaleski wrote that, "Every grazier knows that after his country has been absolutely swept bare of the grey curse there is invariably one here and one there overlooked in some inaccessible places which pop up and start breeding again. Ordinary dogs do not bother with odd ones like these in bad places; but the Beagle, with whom chasing rabbits is an age-old instinct, goes after these "last rabbits" with joy and never leaves them alone until run down and secured."

Nowadays, however, game regulations in parts of Australia differentiate between "hunting with dogs" and "hunting with hounds" and whilst they may be used to "locate and flush out rabbits, hares and foxes", they must not be permitted to "worry, maim or injure animals". Australian fox hunters who use hounds and horses have to be members of an approved hunting organisation and the only hounds permitted to be used for this purpose are bona-fide foxhounds – which have to be identified by a legible ear tattoo and be officially registered. In addition, a means of humane killing must be available to kill a fox if required during a hunt using horses and hounds.

America

Thankfully things are somewhat simpler in North America (although even here, there are certain states where sports such as coursing, for instance, are not permitted). One only has to type the words "rabbit hunting in America" into a search engine in order to find out all there is to know about the subject! As one website commentator has it: "A couple of generations ago, before the great whitetail deer population explosion and before states like Kansas had regular deer seasons, small game hunting ruled supreme, and no animal was more sought after by hunters than rabbits ... and hunting rabbits, the right way and most exciting way, meant using beagles. Not nearly as many hunters pursue rabbits today, but those who do will tell you that it's a whole lot of fun, especially when you throw in a pack of beagles." As a point of interest, it seems that there is also one pack of beagles in Virginia that hunt fox. They are unique in that they are the only hunting beagle pack in the U.S. to be followed on horseback.

Trialing beagles is also very popular in its own right and the American Rabbit Hound Association (ARHA) has more than 170 beagle clubs nationwide that host sanctioned field trials for beagles. The sport has four "divisions": Big Pack, Gun Dog, Little Pack and Progressive Pack. Apparently, fast scenting hounds compete in little pack and big pack; medium-speed hounds in progressive pack, and the "tighter line-control hounds compete in the gun dog division". Make of all that what you will!

SPORT WITH YOUR HOUNDS AND TERRIERS

THE TITLE of this particular chapter suggests all manner of opportunities and experiences – and that is, surely, the attraction of all field sports? Sport with hounds might suggest trail-hunting and rabbiting, whilst with terriers, it could mean a morning's mooching down field edges and hedgerows in search of rabbits, or an evening's frenetic activity in farm outbuildings in search of rats. It could, given the right circumstances and credentials to remain within the Hunting Act, also include the digging out of foxes likely to prove a problem on a game shooting estate – or even using a couple of hounds or terriers to flush a fox towards a waiting Gun.

Mainly, though, the sport with hounds and terriers being discussed in this section appertains to rabbiting and ratting. In some instances, a little pre-hunt checking and reconnaissance might be in order. Obviously it pays to know where the rabbits and rats are likely to be and also, if there's any possible danger of encountering mink or otter along a river bank (and thereby risking falling foul of the stipulations of the Hunting Act), a walk along the intended hunting site a few hours previous and finding no obvious signs of either will prove a useful and precautionary exercise. Such checks can also be used to locate the whereabouts of any farm stock – which could prevent potential problems once your hounds and terriers are out hunting.

LIVESTOCK
All hounds and terriers (indeed all dogs of any breed or type) must be steady to livestock. It might be a somewhat obvious statement but even so, it is

Fig 50: All working dogs must be steady to livestock. Photo: Greg Knight (www.ruralshots.com)

such an important factor that it most certainly warrants a mention before going much further. Sporting dogs must obey certain rules and orders but, above all, they must be steady with livestock otherwise, apart from anything else, you will soon become very unpopular with the farmers and landowners over whose land you are privileged to hunt.

If you are to have peace of mind when out rabbiting and ratting, then you must be certain of the behaviour of your dogs when they are out of sight and if you make an early enough start with accustoming them to livestock, you should have little need to worry for the future. Therefore, as soon as is practicably possible, young dogs must be taken (on a lead) through poultry and among sheep and cattle. It is natural for them to be curious but any more-than-curious behaviour should be curtailed immediately with a sharp tug on the lead and a stern "No!" or, as is sometimes said in hunting circles, "Ware livestock!"

<u>Don't endanger your dog</u>
Whilst it's a good idea to get your hounds and terriers used to livestock, you should always be very aware of the fact that cattle, in particular young cattle, can be dangerous and so great care must be exercised whenever and wherever you are around such beasts.

Generally, when encountering cattle out in the fields, the most sensible thing is to err on the side of caution and keep out of where they are grazing. If this cannot be avoided, keep close to the fence line or hedgerow, never take your eye off the herd and try to have a possible escape route in view. Personally, I would always keep my dogs to heel but unleashed on such occasions as then, should a quick escape be needed, neither you nor your dog is hampered by the lead and it can be a case of every man (and dog!) for themselves.

Of course, hounds or terriers hunting a rabbit might follow their quarry down a hedgerow bordering a field of cattle; in which case it's either a question of leaving well alone (and keeping your fingers crossed), or hoping that early recall training with a horn or whistle proves effective – yet another reason for ensuring that your dogs are responsive to command.

TEACHING DOGS TO JUMP

Terriers are pretty adept at squeezing through the smallest gaps – and bassets and beagles are, quite literally, not too far behind – but you should, nevertheless, train your dogs to jump obstacles and fences cleanly and safely.

Fig 51: Hounds (and terriers) will encounter all types of obstacles out hunting – and need to learn how to jump them cleanly and safely. Photo: Darren Clark

This is particularly important in sheep-grazing areas where square-mesh fencing is often topped off by one, or even two, strands of barbed wire as otherwise injuries and visits to the veterinary surgery are likely to become a regular part of your sporting activities.

In most instances, jumping can be taught by encouragement whilst out on exercise and there are, for example, fallen branches to be encountered. If (safe) obstacles are progressively negotiated, jumping will come naturally but if there is an alley-way between house, outbuildings and/or kennels, it is a simple matter to build some artificial barriers in the passage thus created and (again by encouragement from yourself) teach young dogs to jump over them as part of a game.

Gundog trainers would most likely train their dogs to wait for a command before jumping a fence but with hunting in all its guises, this is not a practical option as there will undoubtedly be occasions when hounds, terriers and members of a bobbery pack are on their own and need to use their initiative. Some early training will, therefore, help prevent accidents.

ENTERING HOUNDS AND TERRIERS

Although a group of hounds or terriers are collectively referred to as a "pack" and hunt as a pack, there are, most obviously, individuals within that pack, each of which have a role to play which helps towards ensuring that, as a group, they have collective success. Some hounds, for instance, might own a scent line more quickly than fellow pack members, whilst some terriers seem keener to catch and kill than they are to scent out their likely quarry and prefer to leave that side of things to others in the pack. Respect and hierarchy are therefore extremely important in any pack situation, whether it be amongst domesticated canines – or the big cats of the African bush. Identifying individual qualities and getting the best from them is an important part of entering both hounds and terriers.

Hounds

Traditionally, young unentered hounds would have been coupled to one in its fifth season when out on exercise and the older dog would hopefully teach the puppy to respond to the huntsman or person in charge. Alternatively two youngsters may have been coupled together, or on two couplings fixed to a single mature hound.

The time taken to accustom youngsters to exercising with established members of the pack will vary. It may take two weeks or two months for a particular pup to realise that it is now part of a group but there is no great rush. Once they are settled, however, they should be allowed out to run with the others and watched carefully to see that they don't develop any undesirable habits.

When the unentered hounds are used to the pack, the final part of their education is by means of a few early morning hunts (known as "Autumn" hunting, or "Training Days"), thus taking full advantage of the fact that the ground will still be damp with dew and therefore more likely to hold a scent. The whole point of the game is to encourage the young entry and when they go back to their kennel, they should do so feeling that the scent (of either an artificial trail or rabbit) is the basis of fun and excitement – they should not, therefore, be kept out so long as to get tired and disillusioned.

As was briefly mentioned above, each young hound will enter at its own pace and shouldn't be rushed: there is a commonly observed rule of thumb that one must never make too early judgement on a young hound. In the case of bassets, they should be given at least three seasons to perfect their skills.

Entering hounds to an artificial line
In a pack, young hounds will learn to own a scent by following their elders and betters but, should there ever be any need to teach one or a couple on their own, the first trails laid should be quite short and when they finish a track and find the source of the scent, be made a fuss of. As they become more proficient, the trails should be made longer, less direct and run through long grass so that there is never any danger of them learning to hunt by sight rather than their noses. The time between the trails being laid and when the hounds are loosed onto it should also become longer.

Fig 52: Unentered hounds soon become used to hunting as members of the main pack after a few early training sessions. Photo: Darren Clark

There's a happy balance to be achieved as you should not make the task too difficult (and risk discouraging a pup), but neither should it be so easy that a young hound becomes bored. It seems to be generally accepted that 20 to 30 minutes between the "runner" laying the scent and hounds "drawing" for it is about right.

Since the Hunting Act, many artificial trails have been experimented with and hounds will hunt most of them but, according to some aficionados, the cry is nothing like as good as when they are on the real thing. The components of an artificial trail scent are quite often a formula kept secret to all but a few: however, I guarantee that it will not be as used by the Berks and Bucks Draghounds back in the 1970s and as described by General John Strawson in his book, *On Drag Hunting* (J. A. Allen, 1999): "The scent chosen was nothing if not original, for wolf droppings supplied by the Master's tame wolves, smartened up by some original ingredients, made what the Hunt called a good cocktail."

HuntingAct.org – "a website for enforcement professionals" – states that "the trail scent purportedly used is animal-based; there is little information on the type of scent used … but in the case of traditional fox hunting packs fox urine is often claimed to be used … in their evidence to the Burns Inquiry, the Masters of Draghounds and Bloodhounds Association stated that their artificial scent trails are generally oil-based …" Interestingly, a beagle pack in South Africa say that, "we do not use artificial scent such as aniseed mixed in oil as we believe our hounds should run on as natural a scent as possible. Our lure is generally made up of a mixture of pilchards and sardines."

NB: *See also On the Trail in Hunting with Others.*

Terriers
The first verse of a Norfolk folksong, *A Setter for the Squire* states:
"A terrier for the labourer
And other simple folk,
For ratting in the stackyard
And rabbits down the yoke."

I would imagine that training young terriers to rats would have been a very simple matter in the days when corn was stacked on the straw and then threshed out during the autumn or winter months. By all accounts, there was never any shortage of rats in the stacks.

Probably the best way of getting a terrier to be proficient at killing rats is by example. Taking a young dog out with experienced ones and letting it

Fig 53: Young terriers learn best from their more experienced elders. Photo: Greg Knight (www.ruralshots.com)

mingle and observe will soon result in the "right sort" very quickly getting the idea and pitching in with as much enthusiasm as the rest of the pack. In any case, where possible, one should always use more than one dog wherever practicable as the more of them that work a rat-infested area, the less likely that any of the quarry will escape.

Aiding education

Rats prefer to live as close as possible to their food and water sources. Any farm environment is obviously likely to be a good bet as there are plenty of easy pickings for the rats and good places for them to hide. Not only does the terrier have the opportunity to kill a rat but, by this method, may learn to use its nose quicker than might otherwise be possible. Always start a terrier off slowly in order that it builds up its confidence in its own time and at its own pace.

You can help by disorientating the resident rat population in a number of ways: an Internet ratting website suggests moving a board or two, placing a cardboard box in a new location and scuffing your heel in a sharp line or two in the dirt to make a little furrow or trench. "All of this serves to alter the rat's visual clues and to break up the invisible but very important scent trails that rats use to 'triangulate' their position." Another possibility is to block as many holes as possible as a disorientated rat which hits a blocked hole will be confused just long enough for the dog to nail it.

During the summer months rats are generally found to have moved away from buildings and taken up residence in the fields and hedgerows. If permission for a walk round these hedgerows can be obtained from the farmer, then presently your terrier is sure to mark a rat to ground. If he also "speaks" to it, so much the better, but he should not be made too excitable or the time may come when he barks as soon as he sees a hole whether it is occupied or not.

The age to begin
Generally, introducing young terriers to a pack out working can be done by taking puppies around the age of three to four months and only allowing them to watch before becoming actively involved at a later date. As to the age at which to actually enter terriers to rats, most modern-day terrier enthusiasts suggest that a pup should have its second teeth. If a young dog gets badly bitten by a mature rat, he will never forget, and until he has his second teeth it is hardly fair to try him. There is a further complication as, before the adult teeth emerge (at the age of around four months), any attempts at killing a rat may involve unnecessary and unsuccessful worrying. This could, in turn, result in the young dog missing more than he kills. The second, but most important thing to consider is the question of leptospirosis, a disease of which rats are known carriers. In humans it is known as Weil's Disease and can prove to be fatal. The same is true with dogs and so it is essential that a terrier which is likely to be doing a fair amount of ratting should be properly vaccinated against this disease (see also Leptospirosis in the Health and Hygiene section of Kennels, Health and Hygiene).

Awakening the "Prey Drive"
American terrier enthusiasts make much of what they call the "prey drive", by which they mean the natural instinct that most influences a dog's working career. Put briefly, it is "the innate or inbuilt desire to hunt".

They explain that the prey drive is "completely separate to the defensive drive (protecting self and pack members) and the sexual/dominance drive (dog-dog aggression)" and is instead, the instinct which sends a puppy after squeaky toys, balls and chasing birds and cats.

In the wolf tribe, a pup would start to follow the pack when still young and learn to hunt by watching its elders and betters. In doing so, it begins to understand what to hunt, where the best places to find its quarry might be, how to approach it, how to run it down and then how to kill it efficiently. The same principles can be adhered to in the training of terriers (and, to

Fig 54: The majority of terriers quickly learn to kill their quarry cleanly and efficiently – but young dogs should be given time before being "entered". Photo: Greg Knight (www.ruralshots.com)

some extent, hounds) but it is important that time is taken in allowing the prey drive to develop as each dog is an individual and shouldn't be rushed for fear of damaging enthusiasm, determination and perseverance.

Training terriers to hunt and quarter

Much of what has been written about entering hounds applies equally as well to terriers in this instance. Much of it is instinct, in fact, unless kept constantly supervised, a terrier will very rapidly become accustomed to taking itself off into the fields and woodlands, following all the scents which instinct tells him that he should. This instinct needs to be channelled – a task often easier said than done!

On the other hand, a terrier which will not hunt through gorse, bramble and other thick cover is not likely to prove of much use when out hunting for rabbits. Fortunately, with a little patience, once a youngster learns that there is something of interest to be found, the rest will come naturally. One should not, however, ever be tempted into pushing or even throwing a dog into thick cover and it ought to be possible to entice him to explore by vocal encouragement or even, as I've seen suggested, with titbits thrown into high, but thornless cover.

Having associated cover with something interesting and exciting, the next step is to get the terrier to hunt to right and left as you walk through the cover so that there is no chance of leaving any rabbits undisturbed. Naturally, most dogs wish to run straight forward instead of quartering the ground but, by walking straight into the wind and moving from left to right yourself, you should soon be able to get the terrier to follow your movements. If it can be arranged so that, dotted on either side of your intended path, there are a few small clumps of bushes, bracken or bramble, the dog's natural inquisitiveness will do the rest. One thing to remember, though, is that it is important to allow the terrier sufficient time to explore these clumps: if you are in too great a rush to get on, the pup will skimp in his hunting for fear of getting left behind.

KEEP CALM AND CARRY ON

Sometimes things do not always go smoothly when it comes to training and entering hounds and terriers. Every dog is an individual and, as we've seen elsewhere, whilst terriers are generally quick to mature, some hounds may take a while before they settle and become important members of the pack.

In most cases it is simply a question of being patient and keeping calm: eventually the penny will drop and everything fall into place in the animal's

Fig 55: Most terriers (including Bedlingtons) will soon lose any fear of cover or water – particularly once they have learned there is sport to be had! Photo: Janine Evans

mind. Any dog trainer will always advise that, if you are not in the right frame of mind, you shouldn't attempt anything but general exercise at such times. It is all too easy to shout and lose ones temper and by doing either, you risk losing the trust of your dog and also causing it to become confused by your actions.

A dog's confidence needs to be built up slowly and naturally. As has been pointed out elsewhere in this chapter, if, for instance, it is wary of water or thick cover there is absolutely nothing to be gained by picking it up and throwing it into either in exasperation. Ditches and shallow water are best broached by setting the pup an example, either by you, or the confident actions of an older, experienced canine companion. Likewise, fences of all kinds are likely to be encountered whilst out hunting and whilst some hounds and terriers will clear an obstacle with the aplomb of a Grand National winner, others will run up and down the fence bottom whining and whimpering. As Penny Taylor, author (Skycat publications), writer, running dogs breeder and expert says: "The easier you make things for young pups, the more confidence they will have, and training a dog is all about starting small and working your way up to serious challenges."

HUNTING RABBITS WITH HOUNDS AND TERRIERS

Once your young hounds and terriers have been "entered" and know exactly what is expected of them, the fun can begin in earnest. Even though you might only have two or three individuals in your "pack" and they might be a motley selection of terrier, beagle, basset or dachshund, there is nothing at all to prevent you from imagining that one is hunting a pack of the finest, noblest hounds in Britain!

To get the best from them, though, there can be no time better spent than going out for a few afternoons' sport with a recognised pack of hounds (of whatever description) in order to watch how their huntsman does things. There is much to observe and learn. Take, for instance, the fact that their hounds will follow quietly at the huntsman's heels until put into cover and told to draw (usually by the use of the words "lieu in!" – which like "view holloa", is another hunting expression derived from the French language).

Optimise your opportunities

For those sportsmen and women who consider the rabbit to be a bit lacklustre when it comes to providing a good run for scenting hounds rather than a

Fig 56: A successful outcome for the Rookley Rabbit Dogs. Photo: Barry Isaacson

quick dash in view of sight hounds, it might come as some surprise to learn that, because of the fact that rabbits would always prefer to use their own particular entrance to their burrow, they will often run past other rabbit's holes looking for their own, thereby creating the possibility for a decent hunt. Rabbits can be surprisingly sporting and hunts of twenty minutes or more can take place. The ground does, of course, need to be of the right sort – there's not much of a run to be had on a close-cropped grass sward alongside a burrow-infested hedgerow. Rough, coarse-grass covered sand dunes, scrub gorse bushes, moorland edges and harvested fields where the stubble has been left long, are all potentially perfect places for an opportunity to watch hounds work after rabbits.

As mentioned below when discussing scenting and weather conditions, the huntsman will, whenever possible, draw upwind so as to give his hounds the best possible chance of picking up any scent, and, in the case of when "live" hunting (permissible within the restraints of the Hunting Act) is being carried out, will most likely stay out of the cover himself so as to be able to see any rabbit that breaks.

Learning from the experience of others

A good "professional" huntsman doesn't always need to keep his hounds in sight as his experience and knowledge of individual hounds will allow him to know exactly what is going on within the cover – quite often simply by listening to the noise his hounds are making.

In a thick spinney or wood, standing outside in the open may be particularly advantageous as, although the sound of the pack might tell him that a rabbit has been found, really dense cover could well mean that the quarry will refuse to break. Eventually, though, it will, in most instances, panic and leave cover – and he will be on hand to see it do so. In their *Rabbiting and Ferreting handbook*, produced many years ago by the British Field Sports Association (which was ultimately amalgamated into what has since become the Countryside Alliance), the co-authors describe such a situation thus: "This was the time to be absolutely alert for the rabbit, finding no peace in cover, would "clap", as the beaglers say, and when the dogs had flashed by, make a bolt across the open. That was the time to get on its line and holloa. They would come dashing out and hit off the line like a pack of foxhounds."

There was also some useful and very pertinent advice given by Colin Haynes in a 1987 issue of *Shooting News* (later to become *The Countryman's Weekly*): "The first couple of drives or hedges you walk up are usually a bit of a disappointment as the terriers dash about here, there and everywhere. If you have a fair bit of work in front of you for the day it is well worth

Fig 57: Rats can be "evicted" from their hedgerow buries with the aid of a smoker – see "Useful Equipment". Photo: Greg Knight (www.ruralshots.com)

coming back later to these first few hedges. Another way to overcome this initial keenness is to walk your terriers before you set off in the morning.

"The normal size brambles present no problems for the average terrier but I sometimes run into a particular sort which seem to hug the ground and reach about two feet high. These brambles are a very slow job as the only place the terrier can go is through the rabbit runs ... a thick old hedge bottom takes a while to work through.

"The best sport to be had is when the buries have been 'stunk out' in February or March. Ground cover is at its lowest and ... a very effective way ... is with small hand-held sprayers filled with creosote. Give each hole a squirt [a day or so before going out hunting] and you will be surprised how many rabbits will be found sitting out."

SCENTING AND WEATHER CONDITIONS
Interestingly, in scientific tests, a dog's nose has been proved to contain four times the amount of olfactory cells than does a human's (some 20 million as opposed to five million!) The outside of a hound's nose is designed to pick up scents: large and wet, it collects and dissolves scent particles for easier identification. Also, when a dog detects a desirable scent, it reacts by salivating, and the wet tongue also helps to pick up and dissolve more scent particles.

Scent itself is made up of microscopic particles. As each quarry type has a distinctive smell, hounds and terriers can distinguish between what is being hunted and any other scents that may have crossed the trail. What an animal is doing can also affect the availability of the microscopic particles that provide its scent. For example, a rabbit's scent is emitted from points between the toes and when initially flushed, more scent is generated when it's on the move. As it tires, though, the scent begins to weaken. The least amount of scent is given off when a rabbit is sitting in its form and from a pregnant female which emits hardly any (presumably as Nature's way of protecting both the mother and her future young).

Weather conditions affecting hunting
In some weather conditions, hounds can pick up an air scent far more easily than they can by running with their noses close to the ground and it is important to realise this just in case you're thinking that a particular animal is running along head held high without contributing anything to the efforts of other members of the pack.

Fig 58: A dog's nose is known to contain four times the amount of olfactory cells than that of a human

Dry air and heat evaporate scent. Rain washes scent away and extreme cold deadens it. Scent clings to soft, moist soil and grass far better than it does to hard, dry ground. Fog and mist make for good scenting, while cold, dry snow does not. Strong winds can scatter scent but neither calm days nor windy days are necessarily best; they are just different.

Ideally, one should always draw upwind wherever possible but even with that help, there are many occasions when scenting can prove difficult for your hounds and terriers. Despite the volumes written on the subject of scent by acknowledged hunting experts such as Peter Beckford and Tom Smith decades ago, despite scientific research, even in the twenty-first century the whole thing continues to be something of a mystery! A famous maxim of Beckford's was: "Take not out your hounds on a windy day" – by which he probably meant to imply that any ground moisture, which is necessary for holding scent, would have been blown away.

Sometimes, what starts as a good scent on grassland, for instance, can often deteriorate if a rabbit runs across a ploughed field or into marshy ground. The explanation put forward in such circumstances is that the grassland is likely to be warmer than the air at the same time that the other type of ground is cooler. Conversely, it could be expected that scenting will be poor when these conditions are reversed and the air is warmer than the ground. There are also certain features likely to cause temporary problems on what would otherwise appear to be a good scenting day, the most obvious being when livestock has foiled the ground. Bracken, dead leaves, and a field of kale or some other strongly scented crop are some further ones whilst artificial fertilisers, chemicals and recent dung-spreading have also been found to be detrimental to the day's sport.

Fig 59: Scenting can be difficult in some conditions – especially in dry, warm autumn weather. Photo: Greg Knight (www.ruralshots.com)

On the morning of a cold, frosty day, scenting conditions may be poor until the sun warms the earth and a fall of snow can certainly affect scenting conditions. However, considering that you will be on foot rather than horse-back, it shouldn't prevent you being able to go out hunting (mounted hound packs will often have to cancel in snowy, icy conditions because of the dangers involved with horses slipping and injuring themselves and their riders).

One thing that one should not be tempted to be when hounds and terriers are struggling with scent, is impatient! As Jack Ivester Lloyd remarked: "The more I see of this hunting with dogs, the more do I agree with the old huntsman's slogan "leave 'em alone". In other words let them work it out for themselves. They know more about the game than you ever will. Your part in the sport is to stand still and enjoy it, 'hollering' them on only to what you are quite certain is the hunted rabbit when they have completely lost it."

"VIEW HOLLOA!"

"View Holloa!" is a term derived from the French and is traditionally used by members of the hunt staff or experienced members of the field to inform the huntsman that they have seen the hunted quarry – "hunted" being the crucial word in this sentence. It shouldn't be used lightly as otherwise your hounds and terriers will soon learn to lift their heads from the line and take a "short-cut" in their hunting by running directly to where the call has come.

There are, however, certain times when a "view holloa" might be necessary and in such circumstances, if members of your pack are going to trust you, they must know that your call (or particular note on a whistle), means only one thing – that you have seen the quarry – so never use it to bring them to you for any other purpose. It is surprising how quickly they learn and, after the first couple of occasions when they have lost "their" rabbit, come to your holloa and found it again, they will soon know the meaning.

As mentioned above, it is, nonetheless, very important not to lift your dogs to a holloa too often as doing so only teaches them to get their heads up and look for help whenever they are at fault.

NB: *For more on the subject of whistles, see also Horns and Whistles in Useful Equipment.*

Fig 60: Avoid the temptation to "lift" hounds and terriers to a "view" – where possible any dog that uses its nose to hunt must be allowed every opportunity to work out a scent on its own.

93

URBAN HUNTING

A few groups of friends mooching with their terriers and lurchers is not a new thing in either the countryside or in town. A mention was made in something written way back in 1851 which described rat-catchers working the streets of London with terriers and ferrets. In modern times, the same thing continues unofficially in the alley-ways of Manhattan, New York (see Introduction) where the Ryders Alley Trencher-fed Society (RATS) hunt with a small pack of assorted terriers. Quite what the local government position is regarding rodent control by such methods is unrecorded as the Health Department of that particular city refuse to comment. Incidentally, in Columbia, Missouri, in April 2013, the first ever rat-tracking/barn hunt trials were held. In this new (and official) American canine sport, terriers get two minutes in which to hunt their way around a hay-bale maze and, as they do so, locate the whereabouts of a live rat held captive in a crush-proof, aerated tube!

The Connaught Square Squirrel Hunt

As an amusing foot-note with which to end this particular section, it is well worth mentioning the Connaught Square Squirrel Hunt (CSSH). The creation of this particular pack consisting of one "hound", a terrier named Dylan, came about in 2005 after Dylan's owner was told by a policeman that if he allowed his dog to chase squirrels in nearby Hyde Park, he could well find himself in breach of the recently enforced Hunting Act. The ridiculousness of it all was not lost on Dylan's owner (nor presumably on Dylan himself as terriers always seem to see the funny side of things!) and so they decided to hold a drag-hunt in gardens near Connaught Square. So popular was the event that, over a period of time, several more "hunts" were held and the CSSH soon had hundreds of subscribers – as well as holding its own Hunt Ball!

KENNELS, HEALTH AND HYGIENE

THERE ARE already many books dealing specifically with the welfare of working dogs of all descriptions – and many websites too. Exactly just how many I'd not really realised until doing a little extra general research. Information appertaining to the kennelling and health and hygiene aspects of hound and terrier keeping is, therefore, readily available: I did, however, think that it might be of value and interest to include the following specific notes.

KENNELS AND KENNELLING

Traditional hound packs do, of course, kennel their dogs outside. Actually, to be more precise, "kennels" are the premises on which hounds are kept; lodges and lodge yards are the buildings in which the hounds sleep and spend their day. Although customarily kept separately in bitch and dog "lodges", some hunts kennel their hounds as a mixed pack. Daphne Thorne of the Barony Bassets tells me that "we kennel them at home in fairly small groups, not divided necessarily by sex but by character and compatibility".

The owner of two or three hounds or terriers who hunt "unofficially" for rabbits and rats (but with the express permission of landowners and/or their tenants) may well consider the options of whether their animals are best kept indoors or out. Most often this decision is a result of practicalities – a few boisterous beagles or grimy Griffons are perhaps not conducive to the typical household's smooth-running – but in other situations, it may be possible to consider whether or not you should keep your working dog indoors as part of the family or kennel it outdoors.

A commonly-held school of thought suggests that a dog under training is better off in a kennel environment because, when out and about with its trainer, it will be focused on its handler (on the other hand, there are also those who feel that a young dog kept within the family environment will be far better "humanised"). Jack Ivester Lloyd's Bagley Rats Hounds lived in the house as members of his family and, writing in the 1960s, he was of this particular opinion: "The theory that a working dog should live out-of-doors and never be fussed may have its good points, but I have yet to discover them. I have known terriers which were what some would call 'spoiled' in their homes but which were little demons for work. I don't care how 'spoiled' my rat and rabbit dogs are at home, so long as they are willing to work until they drop when I take them out."

A compromise might be to use a "cage" as a kennel in the house – which will allow a dog its own secure environment to which it can go to get out of the way of family hustle and bustle. Alternatively, consider an outdoor kennel for the times you are out of the house, but allow your dog(s) access to your home at times suitable to you.

An outdoor kennel can also be useful for the times when dogs are brought in muddy and wet after a day's work – although they should, of course, always be towel-dried before being kennelled, putting them in there for an hour or so will prevent much dirt from finding its way into your home. All outdoor kennels must obviously be dry and draught-proof; preferably with a raised bed both in the sleeping area and in the run. Some manufactured kennels have an option of a covered roof over the outdoor run and are worth considering. Perhaps the most important factor however, is that of security and outdoor kennels should be lockable. A security light and sensor is also a good idea – and even then, never consider your dogs to be completely safe. Only relatively recently, three terriers were stolen from kennels in Oxfordshire and it was the fourth time that these particular premises had been targeted; the owner having had a total of 14 dogs stolen. The animals were housed in secure kennels which were alarmed.

Temper tantrums
As already briefly mentioned above, it is important to consider character and compatibility when contemplating keeping hounds and terriers together as a group. Further ways of avoiding potential problems would be to remember the very valid point raised by author Penny Taylor when she wrote in a *Countryman's Weekly* article that: "For many hunting dogs, those with a higher prey drive than the average pet, summer can be a time of frustration and boredom, and that's without the added annoyance of bitches coming into season when those rising hormones create niggling tension between

Fig 61 above: Many kennel their hounds and terriers outside ... Photo: Greg Knight (www.ruralshots.com)

Fig 62 below: ... whilst many others feel that it does their working dogs no harm at all to be indoors (Darswed Teckels).

previously amicable pack mates. Pack life can provide peace and security but can also be horribly stressful for all concerned at times and it is easy to see why many people who keep dogs in number always kennel them separately."

Even normally placid hounds will occasionally give each other a warning growl and terriers will quite often do that and then follow up immediately afterwards with a scrap! Many breeders and terrier-keepers suggest that no more than two (of opposite sex) should ever be permitted to stay together unattended – advice that will, of course, cause problems when a bitch comes in season. Plenty of exercise will help in avoiding the tendency to fight; as one breeder remarked, "Terriers can be destructive if left unattended and unemployed. Most trouble is due to a lack of discipline, activity and exercise … a tired dog will seldom want to pick a fight."

TRANSPORT
Hounds usually arrive at the meet in a specially designed trailer or specifically dedicated and adapted van. The amateur rabbiting and ratting enthusiast will most likely not have access to such luxury so what is the best way of transporting dogs to and from home?

Most will travel quite happily in the back of a vehicle but the excitable nature of a terrier which has learned through experience that a trip out means sport or pleasurable exercise can be a dangerous liability if it is of the sort that will career round the inside of a car as if it is participating in a "Wall of Death" fairground ride!

It is nowadays possible to buy dog cages to fit in the rear of almost any vehicle – thus ensuring a safe journey for both the dog and its owner. In addition, weatherproof mobile "kennels" can be obtained for fitting into the back of open trucks and, if you have several dogs or are intending travelling a lot with them, a dog trailer or "transit box" could be worth considering. Some

Fig 63: Weatherproof "mobile" kennels can be purchased for use in the back of an open truck – and can be a more discreet colour than this example shows!

Fig 64: For several dogs, a trailer might be worth considering

advantages of the latter are that dogs usually enjoy being in the trailer and feel safe and comfortable; more importantly, the materials used are cool in summer and warm in winter – on top of which is the fact that such trailers offer their occupants good ventilation and visibility.

EXERCISE

Although not hunting during the summer months, it is still important to keep your hounds and terriers in a reasonably fit condition. For most of those who have only two or three dogs living as part of the family, daily exercise is likely to remain pretty constant all the year round but for those with a kennelled pack of several, summer exercise quite often follows a tried and tested regime.

Hounds

The form which exercise takes varies from kennel to kennel but in some of the more traditional ones, there is a large grass run or fenced paddock into which hounds can be put for some self-exercise (quite often whilst the lodges and concrete runs are being swilled out each morning). Sometimes it is possible for the person in charge to take them all out on his own on a daily basis and there can be no doubt that hounds will fare better for one hour's walk each day than they will if circumstances dictate that they can only be exercised two or three times a week for longer periods. Practically, though, large numbers of hounds will require more than just one person to be on hand and so the availability (or otherwise) of willing helpers might well dictate the frequency of such walks.

However, no matter what the time allocated, exercise should be made as beneficial as possible, not only in attaining a hound's peak of fitness, but also as a time to educate and improve their minds. It is particularly important with young hounds and such times can be used to teach them to swim and how to conduct themselves on the road, as well as teaching them to remain still when left unattended – a practice which, once learnt, will be useful on a countless number of occasions. It is best achieved by enlisting help. First of all, get the hounds tightly grouped, then, after giving them an appropriate command, make them stand on their own. Any attempts to follow the person in charge must be checked by their helpers. Thereafter the helpers should all move away slowly but be ready to slip back with a word of warning at the very first sign of movement on the part of any individual animal.

Opportunities for further training will present themselves during hound exercise. After first of all getting the permission of the farmer, hounds can be taken right through the middle of a field (or farmyard) and given the chance to meet at close quarters sheep, young cattle (but beware of young cattle as they can be boisterous and potentially dangerous in a herd when faced by several dogs) and poultry. When taking young hounds amongst these creatures, the huntsman or person in charge should firmly forbid them to take anything other than a cursory interest in their surroundings: by doing so, it will go a long way towards ensuring that potential livestock issues do not become a problem (see also Undesirable Faults in the Hounds and Terriers section and also Livestock in Sport with Your Hounds and Terriers).

Fig 65: Bassets returning from exercise. Photo: Greg Knight (www.ruralshots.com)

Terriers
By their very nature, terriers might not be quite as easy to exercise as hounds! As has been seen in Temper Tantrums above, they do, however, need plenty to keep them mentally stimulated and happy. Most breeds and types do not take at all well to inactive, sedentary lifestyles. A twice daily routine is good but if this isn't possible, a large, fenced area around home may provide an alternative way of providing some exercise, especially if some ball-throwing or similar is included. It is probably best only to leave several terriers in such a run at times when you are within hearing distance as fights may break out due to over-exuberance. The height of fence is also important as terriers are renowned escapologists!

FEEDING
With only a couple of terriers in kennels, their feeding regime is a simple matter but in the case of registered hound packs, or indeed anyone with many canine mouths to feed, how best to do so is another subject entirely.

Traditionalists talk of feeding raw flesh and or tripe – or, as was the case in many hunt kennels when raw flesh was temporarily unavailable – a type of porridge cooked in a boiler in the flesh house. Before the days of health and safety and associated regulations, the hunts provided a useful service to many local farmers by collecting their fallen stock and taking it back to kennels for feeding to the hounds (the sale of skins and bones also give the hunt a little extra revenue) but nowadays things are far more complicated (for example, offal and the like may have to be incinerated on the premises – which are subject to Defra visits and licensing). Some still do, however, feed flesh and many private individuals swear by tripe for their dogs.

A natural diet
There can be no doubt at all that a natural diet is best for any dog, and so one would expect that flesh was best – until that is, one realises that, in the wild, a dog would eat flesh and an animal's intestines, a part of which is the stomach, and which is known as "tripe". The stomach of a rabbit or larger herbivore will obviously contain greenstuff and vegetable matter. Despite how it looks to human eyes, this is nutritious and would form part of a natural diet.

It is a generally accepted veterinary fact that dogs eating a natural, raw food diet can be expected to live longer and suffer less illness and disease. It is, however, not always convenient nor socially acceptable to provide exactly what a dog would eat in the wild in the home environment. Nevertheless, a diet that includes meaty bones, lean muscle meat and internal organs from chicken, lamb, beef, rabbit and pork; eggs, cheese, cottage cheese, yoghurt, milk and butter; and fatty fish such as herring, salmon and sardines can only be beneficial. In addition, consider including plants and root vegetables such as spinach, cauliflower, broccoli, carrots and parsnips. Fresh and dried fruits (but not grapes) are also excellent components of a raw diet.

Sadly, tinned meat is not an easy alternative to fresh: the quality of ingredients in most examples is appallingly low, often including meat that has gone off. "But", one might argue, "surely pack animals in the wild eat such things?" – and so they do; however, the preparation process involves cooking (often at high temperatures) and this kills off vital and extremely important enzymes. Enzymes are chemicals responsible for thousands of internal digestive metabolic processes and if altered from their natural state in any way, are far more difficult for a dog to digest.

In 2014, a newspaper report championed the natural diet and completely decried all other forms of feeding. In particular, it described the manufacturing process of dried food to be "stomach-churning" and claimed that kibbled or dry dog food is created as a result of the ingredients – which, or so the article claimed, is "mostly corn and ground meat" being "heated to a very high temperature and turned into a sort of grey mulch". The reporter (did he taste it, I wonder?!) then went on to opine that result "tastes so foul it has to be sprayed with fat to make it palatable to dogs".

It is, of course, literal "food for thought" but there are undoubtedly situations where feeding a dry food (when away from home, for example) is the only practical solution.

Complete feeds

The manufacturers of complete dog foods have put a great deal of research into the production of their products in order to cater for every taste. There are formulas made suitable for pregnant bitches, newly weaned puppies, fast-growing young stock, working dogs, and retired canines who only need a basic "maintenance" ration in order to keep fit and healthy.

It is vitally important to always obtain freshly manufactured feed – which should be stored in covered containers with tightly fitting lids in a clean, dry, cool area. Always buy your food from a busy store that is known to have a good turnover as by doing so, there is less chance that you will be buying feed which has gone stale or even beyond its "sell-by" date. In general, any manufactured complete meal stored longer than eight weeks is subject to vitamin deterioration and rancidity, especially during the summer months.

The temperature and humidity of where you store your food is also important, as is the need to keep the area clean, well lit and ventilated with fresh air. Store bags on a pallet so that air can circulate and keep the edges of the bags well away from the walls, especially if they are tin, brick or concrete where moisture and condensation is likely to be a problem. Anyone who needs to buy in bulk should also take care not to store more than ten bags on each pallet.

It is also a good idea to design the storage area to facilitate the FIFO (First in First Out) system, with bags stored in consecutive order so that oldest can be withdrawn first – it is too easy to empty the place nearest to the door, replenish that space with "fresh" food and then use that first again – leaving older bags to go stale at the back of the building.

HEALTH AND HYGIENE

Continually improving drugs (particularly antibiotics and vaccines) as well as surgery techniques has made life much easier for both general dog owners and the owners of working dogs. The latter, are, because of what they do, far more likely to receive cuts, injuries and leg strain. Injection times, for example, can be used to let the vet see each animal for a thorough check-up, especially with regard to teeth, eyes and ears. Likely sources of infection are also to be found at this stage and the eyelids can be examined for hidden thorns, the lower lids for dust and weed seed. Cataracts and warts may also be noticed for the first time and, if they are likely to cause impaired vision, your vet may suggest that they need to be surgically removed.

Regular booster injections should be given annually – especially in the case of terriers which are prone to picking up leptospirosis because of coming into contact with

Fig 66: Injection times can be used to let the vet look for hidden thorns, weed seed and cataracts in the eyes.

Fig 67 left: Booster injections should be given regularly ...

Fig 68 below: ... and worming is also extremely important. Both photos: Greg Knight (www.ruralshots.com)

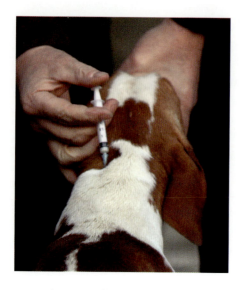

rats during the course of their sporting activities. Worming is also extremely important as, particularly where hounds are kept in traditional circumstances, transmission of these internal parasites is facilitated by the aggregation of large numbers of dogs sharing grass exercise runs (every effort must be made to clear such runs of excrement on a regular basis).

Ticks

Because of the type of cover through which they hunt and work, the hunting hound or terrier is probably more liable to becoming a host to ticks than is the average pet. As is well known, ticks are carriers of several diseases, Babesiosis (Lyme Disease) and Piroplasmose being just two. Leaving the tick attached to the skin of a dog for any length of time might well result in an exchange of blood between tick and host and doing so may just possibly cause a transmission of disease if that particular tick happens to be a carrier. Removing ticks by the various old wives' methods is not, however, generally recommended and although many people swear by the application of petroleum jelly, lighter fluid and the like in the perceived hope that it will

Fig 69: Ticks can cause serious problems if left to feed from its host for any length of time.

either cause the tick to lose its grasp or actually suffocate, it is nowadays thought that such remedies may well cause the tick to disgorge the contents of it's stomach directly into the host's bloodstream, thus further increasing the chance of infection.

Mites and allergies

Mites are often so small that a veterinarian will require a microscope to make an unmistaken identity. Harvest mite larvae, which can be recognised as clusters of orange/red dust attached to the dog's hair, can cause severe problems and an unhappy animal. Itching develops in a dog within about half a day of exposure, but the discomfort can continue for several weeks. Itching can, apparently, be relieved by Omega 3 and 6 oils and there are also several proprietary treatments, including creams and sprays, that help clean up the irritation and encourage the healing process – as well as providing protection from bacterial infection.

Parasites of any description are the most common source of skin problems in dogs and, due to all the scratching and rubbing that an animal will do in order to relieve itself by itching, many secondary problems may arise. Allergies are another common cause of skin problems. A dog, like a human, can be allergic to almost anything, but some common causes of allergies in dogs are pollen, dust, mould and grass, with which all working dogs come into regular contact. Canine skin allergy symptoms include rashes, very itchy skin, scratching constantly, rubbing the muzzle and often chewing on their paws. Others may have ears that feel hot to the touch. It is possible to have your vet conduct an allergy test and once the cause has been identified, it may be practicable to remove it from the dog's every day life. If, however, the allergy is from things that are uncontrollable such as pollen, grass and mould spores, the veterinarian can arrange to have an "antigen" made up specifically for the dog. This is almost always administered by injection and can show quite dramatic results.

Leptospirosis

The sport of ratting with terriers leaves them susceptible to disease. Rats can, apparently, transmit as many as 35 diseases to canines and humans, the most common of which is leptospirosis (which is known as Weil's Disease when it affects humans). Any type of dog should be fully inoculated but as far as terriers likely to be coming into regular contact with rats are concerned, their inoculations must always be most effective against leptospirosis. It is interesting to note that nearly every type of livestock (including humans) can be made very ill by catching leptospirosis – ironically, a rat is immune and will remain unaffected. Possible symptoms include listlessness, unquenchable thirst, putty-coloured faeces and a yellowing of the eyes. If you ever think that either you or your dog might be suffering from leptospirosis (aka *leptospiral jaundice*) then it is imperative that you see a doctor or vet at the earliest opportunity.

Take as many precautions against catching the disease as you can. These include trying to prevent your dog from drinking from puddles in which there is a danger that rats may have urinated and not allowing a dog to "mouth" a rat once it has killed it. As far as you are concerned, it will pay to wear gloves whilst handling pallets, straw bales and other items found in a barn environment and on which rats may have urinated. You should also wear them if you are intending moving rat carcases once killed – but, where practicable, it is far better to do so with a shovel or even, as I've seen used on a couple of occasions, a set of robust salad tongs.

Fig 70: Terriers used for regular ratting expeditions must be inoculated against leptospirosis. Photo: Greg Knight (www.ruralshots.com)

Kennel cough

Kennel cough (a highly contagious respiratory infection in dogs) is the scourge of many a hunt kennel and can put a stop to hunting days and attending shows. Quite often, if just one dog in a kennel has the infection, the rest will probably get it overnight and unfortunately even dogs vaccinated against kennel cough can catch it (see Vaccinations below). Due to the high level of risk, strict isolation measures must be implemented as soon as any indication of a possible problem is noticed.

As kennel cough can be spread by airborne particles, infected isolated animals should not share the same space as other dogs but be completely walled off – a situation that is obviously not always practicable, but should, nevertheless, be considered. The use of a foot-bath – the disinfectant solution in which should be regularly changed and always kept up to strength – is another consideration, as is the use of disposable gloves and overalls at the entry to the isolation area. Routine kennel cleanliness is also important: scrubbing down with a proprietary disinfectant will help in killing off the bacteria which causes kennel cough.

Injuries and Wounds

Despite the ever present possibility of leptospirosis, most rat-inflicted wounds are minor and can be carefully washed and dressed with iodine

Fig 71: Routine kennel cleanliness is important. Photo: Greg Knight (www.ruralshots.com)

or an anti-bacterial ointment. Other possible injuries likely to affect both terriers and hounds include general cuts and wounds. In most cases they will heal easily if treated in a methodical and sensible way – the whole secret is to keep them spotlessly clean (sometimes easier said than done!), and on no account should one let them begin to heal until they are completely clean.

If a wound requires stitching it should be done as soon as possible after the accident, but it must be remembered that stitching a deep wound may prevent dirt from getting out. When stitching is undertaken the lowest part of the wound should always be left open as a drain. Wounds must, therefore, heal from the inside towards the outside; if the outside heals first there is always a chance that it may become septic. The most troublesome are those which might best be described as punctures. They are almost always deep and there is only a very small surface area.

Dealing with minor injuries
It is always worth checking your dogs when returning from a day's hunting. The eyes are a good place to start in case of damage from briars or seeds. Then look carefully for signs of any minor wounds – which can be cleaned with diluted Savlon and subsequently have Aloe Vera or Tea Tree Oil gel applied: both are antibacterial.

Green clay powder is more commonly used as a human facial or body preparation but I have heard of several owners of working dogs who keep it in the kennel medicine chest due to the fact that it is supposed to help in preventing scarring after injury, drawing out impurities and, when mixed with water, is beneficial as a poultice. Those who have used it in the latter instance say that it will "draw amazing amounts of poison, pus and dead tissue from a wound" and recommend that the mixture is mixed and kept in the fridge prior to being applied as "the relief the cold clay brings to an inflamed wound is much better when chilled". I would, however, suggest talking to your veterinary surgeon first.

<u>Poison problems</u>
Whilst we are all careful not to let our dogs have access to obvious poisons, there are some less obvious sources which could, at the very worst, prove fatal. Some of the most common forms of non-caustic poisons include agricultural chemicals, dressed seed and antifreeze – all of which might be found in farm buildings in which one is ratting. As to antifreeze, it might be argued that no dog in its right mind would willingly lap up any which has

Fig 72: Accidental poisoning can result from the most mundane of sources.

been spilt but it is, apparently, quite sweet-tasting and, judging by the entries on some veterinary computer records, is a regular source of poisoning.

Caustic poisoning is likely to occur from the likes of kerosene, battery acid, barbiturates and acetic acids. If the poison has not been taken internally, and it is only on the skin or feet for instance, there is no need to worry unduly but, nevertheless, a careful eye should be kept on the dog in case it begins to lick off the poison before there is any chance of washing it off. Should a hound or terrier have ingested it, however, then it is generally thought that the poison should be diluted whilst in the stomach by giving milk in the case of an acidic poison or, for those of an alkaline nature, a solution of vinegar or lemon juice. Trying to make a dog sick, whilst okay for non-caustic poisons, is not considered to be a good idea because the passage of the poison back through the trachea and soft palate will re-aggravate the situation.

Snow affecting the pads of hounds and terriers
Sometimes hunting or indeed simply exercising in snow can cause ice-balls to form between a dog's paws; particularly in those types that have long or wire hair. To help prevent this from happening, some people like to keep the hair between the paw pads short so that it is even with the pad. Cesar Millan, the original "Dog Whisperer", recommends that this hair should be trimmed in order to make sure none of the hair comes into contact with the ground as it will, he says, "help prevent ice balls from forming between and around the paw pads which can be painful and result in trauma". Millan also reckons that although keeping a dog's nails trimmed is important year-round, it is even more so in the winter "because long nails force the paw to splay out and make it more likely that snow and ice will accumulate between the paw pads".

In prolonged periods of snow, it might even be an idea to apply a dressing of Vaseline or anything lanolin-based such as the creams and balms that might be applied to a cow's udder after milking. Hounds and terriers kept in

Fig 73: Hunting in the snow might be an interesting experience – but beware of ice-balls forming in the pads of wire-haired breeds. Photo: Darwed Teckels

cold kennels ought at least to have their feet wiped with a cloth wetted with warm water so as to remove snow, ice and ice melt after being out in harsh conditions for any length of time. If ice-balls are left in such situations, there is a possible danger of frost-bite.

VACCINATIONS

The most basic of vaccines protects against the three fatal viral diseases distemper, hepatitis and parvovirus. It is also possible to use a vaccine that also includes protection against a viral form of kennel (canine) cough and there is another for the bacterial form of kennel cough. Vaccines are available to protect against canine coronavirus and leptospirosis (see above). What are known as "C3" vaccines can be given to pups once at ten weeks of age and will require boosters every three years. Annual vaccination against kennel cough (see above) is still required. Which vaccine is used depends on your situation and your vet's advice.

ORGANIC AND HERBAL
"I much prefer to give medications and chemicals a wide berth and instead use natural remedies and preventives whenever possible," so says one huntsman of my acquaintance. Just exactly how these natural solutions work depends on the type but garlic, for instance, is known to have an effect only on pathogenic (i.e.; "bad") bacteria and not on the more positive *lactobacillus* types. In addition, it has antiviral properties and acts as an appetite enhancer, an aid to digestion and is also a natural repellent of fleas. It is put to regular use by horse breeders, chicken-keepers and dog owners alike.

Garlic granules can nowadays be bought as a supplement but you could simply crush cloves of fresh garlic in a press. Expressing the juice and crushing the flesh of the clove releases the active ingredients and including just a small amount to a dog's biscuit allowance, adding hot water and then letting it soak for a couple of hours before mixing it all in with the animal's main meal can do nothing but good. As a rough guide, this mix should be prepared every three days for an adult dog.

SOME NOTES ON BREEDING
Whilst this is only ever intended to be a book covering the subject of trail-hunting and hunting rabbits and rats with hounds and terriers, a few general notes on the selection of stud dogs and brood bitches, mating, pregnancy and puppies might prove useful to some.

Apart from the established packs who obviously have both bitches and dogs (possibly from several unrelated or line-bred bloodlines) in their kennels, it is most likely that the person who hunts with just a couple of hounds or terriers will stick with either bitches or dogs – depending on their personal preference – and will either take a bitch to a suitable stud dog to mate, or buy in a puppy or two when the time comes for young stock, an increase in numbers, or sadly, replacements for old "veterans". Having said that, out of interest, I do know of two private packs of registered hounds where only bitches are kept and whenever a litter of pups might be required, the owners make use of a stallion hound from elsewhere.

Selecting the right stock
Obviously any hound or terrier from which you are considering breeding should be as close as possible to any breed standards wherever appropriate. In other situations where there may be no hard and fast rules, there are

still certain requirements that are accepted as being desirable; such as, for example, a size of dog perfect for the terrain and surroundings in which it is likely to be worked.

I have two books on the subject of breeding open in front of me. Both are written by experts well qualified to put pen to paper, and yet they vary in their opinions. One tells the reader that he should: "... be careful to select as parents, both dog and bitch with a line of ancestry as nearly as possible of the height at which you are aiming ... it is unwise to breed from hounds lacking in symmetry and beauty, however well they perform ... Of the two, I consider the dog of far greater importance ..."

Whilst the second states that: "Many breeders are prone to select their bitches rather at random, though they pay ever so much attention to the stallion hound to which they put them. This must be a mistake, as the bitch probably plays at least as big a part in the make-up of the progeny as does the dog."

It is obviously necessary to have some knowledge of an individual's particular breeding – a hound list or pedigree papers are the best way but these are not always available. Those who are building up a pack should try

Fig 74: Old pedigree papers and stud books are fascinating – and extremely useful when considering possible breeding options.

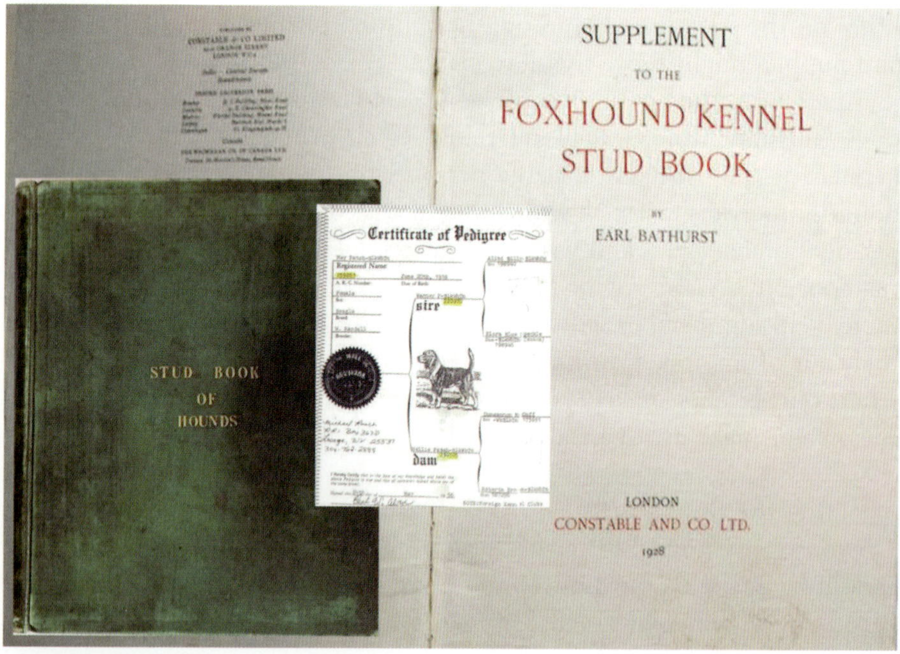

and collect several female lines and keep them going for as long as possible, for the more there are, and the more different ways back there are to them, the closer it is possible to breed within the home kennel.

Out-crossing (whereby a bitch is taken to an unrelated dog) is perhaps the most common method of breeding. Line-breeding involves the mating of related dogs in an attempt to increase or concentrate the homogeneous qualities of a few individuals. Unless carefully controlled it is not long before line-breeding becomes in-breeding, a most undesirable practice which brings to the surface bad characteristics more often than it does good ones and also tends to lower stamina, resistance to disease, and decreases size and bone structure. The closer in-breeding is practiced, the more likely it is that these failures will develop and future offspring's working ability will suffer as a result.

General observations

Ideally, one obviously wouldn't choose to breed from a terrier lacking gameness (see Undesirable Faults in the Hounds and Terriers section), nor a dog which, as briefly mentioned above, is not of a size and stamp likely to produce offspring suitable for the topography and type of hunting intended. Those might be obvious pointers but what about considering a dog's intelligence before deciding whether or not to breed from a particular individual? An intelligent hound will (without "skirting") work a way through or round an obstacle logically and an intelligent terrier will know exactly where and when to dart in and take hold of a rat or rabbit without risking getting bitten or kicked by a rabbit's powerful back legs. In pre Hunting Act days when it was permissible for far more people to enter their terriers to foxes underground, some of the best workers to be seen had hardly a scar or bite on them due to being intelligent enough to keep close to, but not within biting distance of a fox.

WHELPING AND PUPPY-CARE

As far as the actual care of a bitch in whelp and the after-care of puppies are concerned, there is no real need to go into any depth. Any book on the general welfare of dogs will advise the reader and, after all, the way in which a puppy is formed and born differs not in the slightest no matter whether the parents are chihuahuas or wolfhounds!

TAIL-DOCKING

Although I think it important to include the subject of tail-docking in a book which concerns itself so much with the subject of terriers, I urge the reader to continually check the latest situation as, in some aspects of current law, further legislation may mean changes. At the time of writing, the information contained within this section is, to the best of my knowledge, correct.

The Animal Welfare Act 2006 introduced wide-ranging provisions against neglect and cruelty, but the most important for hunting folk relates to tail docking. In England (not Scotland; where a complete ban was introduced in April 2007) there is now an official exemption allowing the tails of some sporting breeds (spaniels, hunt/point/retrieve breeds and terriers) to be docked legally by a vet as long as requirements for proof of a working career are met. The puppy must be docked before it is five days old. The Welsh legislation is similar to that in England (technically, the docking of dogs' tails has been banned there since 2007), except that the breeds that can be docked are named specifically, and the docking of cross-breeds is unlawful – a factor that might prove complicated if one wishes to dock a non-pure terrier type. In Northern Ireland, where legislation similar to that imposed in Scotland was originally decreed, the Assembly voted in 2011 (as part of their Welfare of Animals Act 2011) to exempt certain working dogs after animal welfare issues were raised.

If you buy a puppy with a docked tail, make sure that the breeder gives you the necessary official paperwork – normally a certificate signed by their vet.

TATTOOS

Finally in this section, my mention of the traditions of French hounds elsewhere (see Collars, Leads and Couplings in Useful Equipment) reminded me

Fig 75: At the time of writing, the tail-docking of some working breeds is legal in England and Wales (but not Scotland).

of the fact that most of the hounds you will see out in France are actually marked with a quite prominent brand indicating the name of the hunt. These are usually on the flanks of the hound and obviously freeze-branded there when they are puppies. However, as far as I can make out, freeze-branding is illegal in the UK and is, therefore, not an option.

Traditionally, hounds which belong to registered packs have always been tattooed inside their ear. These tattoos almost always include the initials of the hunt and quite often, other identification numbers or marks as well. Opinion in the hunting world as to the efficaciousness of tattooing as against the implanting of a micro-chip (again, see Collars, Leads and Couplings in Useful Equipment) is divided, with several being against the practice of tattooing for hounds or terriers. Those in favour feel that a dog can be instantly recognised – and tattooing is the cheaper option – whilst those against cite problems with identifying a particular tattoo as the animal ages and, of course, the possible cruelty aspect of using a tattooing kit.

Micro-chipping and registration is, in their opinion, the better way and, although a micro-chip is not obvious if a dog strays or is stolen, point out that it is nowadays standard practice for veterinary surgeons and animal shelters to check for the presence of a micro-chip with a scanner.

Fig 76: French hunting establishments identify their hounds by a form of freeze-branding – but micro-chipping is surely the modern way ... and will be a UK legal requirement in early 2016.

Micro-chipping legislation

Government figures have it that over 100,000 dogs of all types are either dumped or lost each year, at a cost of £57 million to animal charities and local authorities and so, in an effort to combat this, a new piece of legislation comes into effect in 2016. A change in the law will make it a legal requirement for all dogs to be micro-chipped – with chips that contain coded details of ownership. Owners who do not comply could face fines of up to £500.

WHAT TO WEAR

AT THIS POINT, some thoughts and ideas regarding what to wear are well worth a mention. Being suitably attired can make the basics of kennel husbandry more practicable – as can wearing clothes which, depending on the time of year, make things more comfortable. There are, for instance, shirts, trousers, fleeces, jackets, socks and caps made to be tick-resistant and therefore of real value during the periods when ticks are likely to be active. Such clothing is, apparently, equipped with this tick-resistant protection during manufacture and is, according to the company (Rovince), a patented impregnation of "ZECK-Protec" which is "odourless, skin-friendly, UV-proofed and machine washable". Clothing protected in such a way seemingly "needs no further treatment in its lifetime".

Generally, though, in the types of hunting mainly covered within these pages, there is no real need to buy specific clothes and keeping dry, warmth and practicality is what the hunting wardrobe is all about. Whether you are following a recognised pack of hounds hunting an artificial trail, a "bobbery" pack out after rabbits, or are likely to be standing for hours on end whilst terriers do their stuff round a draughty farm building, are all factors to consider in your choice of clothes. Whatever you wear should, of course, be well-fitting and offer the correct amount of mobility necessary for whatever it is you are undertaking.

The same clothes that are wonderful for standing around in can cause the wearer to soon become uncomfortable if they are running after hounds in full flight so dressing in layers that can be removed is not a bad idea if you are at all likely to be involved in the latter scenario. You do then, of course, have the added hassle of carrying around whatever it is you've just removed but that's probably a minor inconvenience compared to being over-heated!

Fig 77: It can be a cold business observing hounds work from the top of a hill in winter – water and windproof clothing is a must!

COATS AND JACKETS

Any clothing suited (no pun intended!) for any outdoor field sports activity should keep you dry and warm. A somewhat obvious statement but the choice is as bewildering as it is useful. "Gore-tex" and "Teflon" treated coats and soft Loden jackets all help in keeping out the wind and rain and all breathable fabrics are brilliant in ensuring that you get neither too hot nor cold and work by wicking away moisture. A fleece, worn under a jacket on the coldest day, or a gilet in place of a jacket on the warmest, is also a useful addition to your wardrobe.

Look out for names such as "Musto", "Barbour", "Schoffel" and "Seeland": taking care to read the attached labels carefully so as to reassure yourself of the following two things:
1) That you know exactly what materials the clothing is made from and whether it is likely to prove fit for purpose.
2) That, when the time comes, you can clean it (or have it cleaned) according to the manufacturer's cleaning and storing advice – which should be on the label.

One for the ladies!
Some shooting jackets are made with the female form in mind – and most are equally suitable to wear watching hounds at work on a cold, wet

and windy day. One company (Outfox) has taken things a stage further and offer a hunting suit "tailored and designed for the feminine figure". According to their publicity blurb, "The range features a removable, scent-reducing 'Ergotarn' lining that allows you to get closer to the quarry and hunt upwind." Possibly designed more with female deer stalkers in mind, there might be occasions when such technology could prove useful out hunting with hounds and terriers.

"Camo" gear

There are probably many who would disagree with me, but I have to say that I'm not a lover of camouflage-patterned jackets (or even over-trousers). There may be certain field sports such as pigeon-shooting where such items of apparel might prove necessary (and even when taking wildlife photos) but in the general scheme of things with regards to the type of hunting discussed in this book, warm and practical though they may be, I think they often give the wrong impression to onlookers. Appearances shouldn't matter, but they do and I know that the general public is often suspicious of wearers of "camo" gear thinking – quite erroneously – that they have something to hide about their sport. Similar thoughts might also enter the heads of any farmers and landowners should you choose to wear such clothing when approaching them for permission to go rabbiting or ratting.

SHIRTS AND UNDERCLOTHES

Warm country shirts (often of the design known as "Tattersall") are ideal for most days out with hounds and terriers. Whatever sort you choose, make sure that the cuffs do not protrude from those of your coat or jacket: wet cotton shirt cuffs can turn cold quickly on a wet day and create a chill throughout the wearer's body.

Under-layers should be made of wool or some type of modern synthetic material that, like socks (see below under Boots and Wellingtons), stays warm when wet, or repels moisture from the body. Like the wet cuffs of a shirt, moisture (whether it comes from the elements or as a result of perspiration) can turn cold very quickly during any period of inactivity. For this reason, I would suggest that polo necks such as those sold in shooting shops might solve the subject of shirt and under-layers in one fell swoop. For really cold days, thermal underwear manufactured by the likes of Damart is very definitely a worthwhile investment.

BREECHES AND TROUSERS

Best of all are the modern shooting trousers and "plus twos" which, unlike the tweed of old, does not scratch and irritate your legs. Outwardly, the material feels soft to the touch, but despite that, the best are waterproof, windproof and breathable. Another alternative might be a pair of climbing breeches, but if you go down this particular route, it is as well to ensure that they are not cut so tight as to restrict your movement should you need to run or walk briskly – the requirements of a climber are not necessarily the same as those of a hunter.

Waterproof leggings

In America, many rabbit hunters wear heavy canvas bib overalls to protect them from thorny thick cover when drawing through with their hounds and terriers but for most of us, either a pair of traditional waterproof leggings such as those made by Barbour, or a pair of the thornproof/waterproof trousers which seem to be increasing in favour with deer stalkers and beaters on British shoots, will suffice.

These latter alternatives are, I must admit, pretty good. They have been popular in France for quite a number of years and are used by rough shooters and those who work their terriers to fox and badger underground. They are now readily available in the UK from almost any and every rural sports or agricultural suppliers.

Fig 78: "Plus twos" and a pair of warm shooting socks are a good combination for any time spent watching hounds and terriers at work.

OVERALLS AND KENNEL COATS

Also in France, members of the various terrier-digging clubs (which are quite legal and strictly regulated over there) might also wear a set of work overalls, many of which sport the name of their particular club or group on their backs. Overalls are, of course, a sensible way of keeping that little bit cleaner than might otherwise be possible when digging in wet clay and similar soil conditions, but they're also well worth considering for use in dirty barns and farm buildings when ratting in this country. In addition, they are very effective as insulation on a cold and windy day!

It is possibly worth investing in a set of nylon overalls for use in kennels if you have several runs to swill out and disinfect on a daily basis – I've lost count of the number of times that, in the days when I used to be involved with hunt kennels, I ended up with half a bucket full of water down my wellingtons! Traditionally, hunt staff would wear brown kennel coats to carry out their daily chores and exercise hounds out on foot and even now wear white kennel coats (complete with bowler hat!) when showing off their new entry on the flags at the annual puppy show.

While kennel coats might keep the wearer clean, I doubt that they are of any practical use when it comes to preventing the transmission of bacteria.

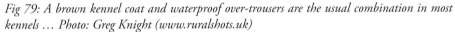

Fig 79: A brown kennel coat and waterproof over-trousers are the usual combination in most kennels ... Photo: Greg Knight (www.ruralshots.uk)

Fig 80: … whilst a white coat (and bowler!) is the order of the day at the annual puppy show. Photo: Greg Knight (www.ruralshots.uk)

Nylon coveralls might, though, and they are light to wear and relatively cheap to buy. They are waterproof but breathable, soft but tough. Most have a full-front zipper and legs and arms have elasticized cuffs. Coveralls of this nature can be washed and disinfected but are economical enough to be discarded after only being worn once in the unfortunate event that something like kennel cough (see Health and Hygiene in the previous chapter) means extra vigilance and precautions need to be taken. They can be purchased at almost every agricultural suppliers.

BOOTS AND WELLINGTONS

Boots ought to be tough enough to ward off thorns and be waterproof, at least on the bottom around the welt. Like any item of clothing, leather ankle boots take some time to wear in and feel really comfortable. Once a pair of leather boots have been properly broken in, it pays to look after them in the hope that they will give years of protection and comfort. To that end, always remove the worst of the dirt and mud straight away and, if they are wet, stand them to dry out naturally in a warm airy place: don't, however, be tempted into placing them too close or even on top of a stove or radiator. Special bags of crystals that absorb moisture can be bought and these help to wick away the dampness from inside the boots. These bags must then be dried out before using them again. Failing that, the old traditional standby of using scrunched up newspapers stuffed inside boots certainly helps in absorbing wet resulting from walking through an over-deep puddle or stretch of water.

As far as Wellingtons are concerned, there are several manufacturers who specialise in creating quality, natural rubber boots designed expressly with the field sports person in mind. Long gone are the days of sloppy, ill-fitting farmer's boots and most by the likes of "Le Chameau" or "Aigle" incorporate a fitted design around the ankle and lower leg. Some are leather or Gore-tex lined for extra warmth and comfort – and may also have the added refinement of a full-length or part-length strong YKK zip down the side, which makes both getting into and out of them, a great deal easier than it is with conventional Wellingtons. You do, of course, have to pay for the privilege and such boots are not, when compared to other makes, particularly cheap.

Somewhere between a Wellington and leather boot is the calf-length leather Wellington boot! Possibly the best known of these is the Dubarry which is made from Drifast-Drisoft leather and is Gore-tex lined. They, and boots of a similar type, generally have a suede appearance and, as such,

Fig 81: A pair of Wellingtons might be the order of the day when out ratting. Photo: Greg Knight (www.ruralshots.uk)

require a little careful maintenance from time to time – nothing too onerous, just a careful rub with an old towel and the application of a protector spray. Other types may need special cleaners and conditioners – all of which are produced by the boot manufacturers themselves. Personally, I'm a recent convert to Toggi country boots: they are waterproof, well-fitting, warm and comfortable – and look smart enough for any occasion.

If you're following a trail-hunting pack such as beagles and bassets in trainers – as many do – always take with you a change of socks and shoes. It is almost certain that your feet will get wet and muddy, which is both dangerous and uncomfortable when it comes to the end of the day and it is time to drive home. Generally, socks should be wool, or made of some synthetic fabric that stays warm even if your feet get a bit damp.

Boot bags

If your family car is likely to double up as transport for your various hounds and terriers then you are likely to be fighting a losing battle when it comes to keeping its interior clean of mud and countryside-associated debris! If, on the other hand, you are a "watcher" more than a participant and you've only yourself to transport from A to B, then it might pay to buy a boot bag in which you can stash muddy boots and Wellingtons for the journey home. If nothing else, it will help maintain domestic harmony and there's no worry of wet mud or water seeping into the vehicle's upholstery. There are several manufacturers of such products and it should be possible to purchase a boot bag for about £20.00 – money well spent in the all-important quest for marital bliss!

HATS, GLOVES AND SCARVES

In the countryside, for any manner of sporting activities, the flat cap is perfect and is probably the headgear of choice for almost everyone involved in hunting and working dogs. Its one disadvantage is that it does not keep your ears warm. A woolly hat (preferably in a dark, subdued "country" colour) will solve this problem and, unlike a trilby or any similar hat with a brim, is not likely to blow off when you're standing on an exposed hillside on a blustery winter's day.

As far as gloves are concerned, thin cotton ones are usually sufficient and will keep your hands from being directly exposed to the cold air on dry days. Leather shooting gloves are also good on such days and, if of a correct fit, should be like a second skin. They are not much good when it is raining, though, as they quickly get sodden and your hands very cold. When it's wet, fingerless wool or polypropylene gloves might be a better alternative. Although mention has been made of surgical gloves being included in a first-aid kit (see Ideas for a First-aid Kit in Useful Equipment), in addition to that, they are one of handiest things to have around the kennel. They are great hand protection for any chores involving water, food preparation and applying any necessary ointments and sprays. If you buy them in as large a size as possible (they are cheap enough to buy by the box), surgical gloves can even be worn over lightweight "proper" gloves in the winter and make a big difference in keeping your hands clean and dry, which helps keep them warmer.

A hunting stock has many a practical use (see immediately below) and will certainly protect its wearer from rain trickling down the neck. For others, a light scarf might prove practical (avoid large bulky ones which will get in the way of movement), but possibly the best way of ensuring a warm, dry neck is to use a towelling shooting cravat which keep you warm even when it is rain-soaked.

A WORD ABOUT HUNT UNIFORMS

Those involved with recognised packs of beagles and bassets might very well wear some sort of hunt uniform but there are some who nowadays play down the formal attire because of not wanting to draw unwanted attention from non-hunting members of the public. Although not directly connected with the type of sport described in this book it is, nevertheless, interesting to note the comments of Jill Mason in her excellent and wonderfully researched tome, *Away, My Lads, Away*. "... a Fell huntsman during the twentieth century would have traditionally worn a red jacket, waistcoat and brown breeches ... But all this changed ... when the Central Committee of Fell Packs decided that discretion might be the better part of valour ... Unlike the lowland packs fell huntsmen now go about their business in mufti with their smart red jackets relegated to the wardrobe only being retrieved for shows and official occasions." Those in charge of "formal" yet private packs of rabbit-hunting and ratting packs ought to look smart and many, depending on the time of year, will wear moleskin trousers, shirts, ties and waistcoats.

Elsewhere, most of the clothing which members of the hunt staff wear has a practical purpose. Some may wear a tie but, in cases where a hunting stock is favoured, on a wet day it will prevent water from running down the wearer's neck and, in the unlikely event of an accident, can be used as an emergency bandage. The hunt coat serves not only to protect the wearer from the cold and wet but also identifies them as being an obvious officer of the hunt to the followers and subscribers. Customarily, the coat is green in colour for most packs of beagles and bassets but it may vary. The Warwickshire Beagles, for instance, wear a mulberry colour and the Westerby Bassets, one of mustard corduroy. The Albany and West Lodge Bassets buck the trend even further by not only wearing bright yellow, but fleeces instead of the traditional hunting jacket. Breeches are almost always white – not necessarily an ideal colour when one considers muddy paw-prints, but a very practical way of seeing members of the hunt staff from a distance.

Fig 82: White breeches are not necessarily the most practical of colour - but they do enable hunt staff to be seen from a distance.

BAGS AND RUCKSACKS

Again it depends on what you are doing but there are times when it might prove useful to carry a light bag or rucksack into which items of clothing can be stuffed when not needed. Dog leads and odd bits of sporting paraphernalia can also be stored as, of course, can a pack of sandwiches and a thermos of tea, coffee or soup.

If you are likely to be indulging in any hunting activity which is likely to involve running around or sudden quick movements, I would suggest that a small rucksack should be your preferred option as it is less likely to flop and slide about than would a game bag or similar which is simply slung over the neck and one shoulder. There are plenty of types available and one only has to spend but a few minutes searching the Internet in order to find many and varied designs aimed at all pockets.

Now, whether you would describe a rucksack or bag as being an item to wear, or whether it is actually a piece of equipment is open to discussion. Should you think it the latter; it leads beautifully onto the subject of "Useful Equipment" which features in the next section!

USEFUL EQUIPMENT

FOLLOWING ON from the last chapter, a designated rucksack or game bag is a useful item in which to keep small, sundry items of equipment such as leads, a pair of gloves, small first-aid kit – for you and your dogs – and even a tube of insect repellent for those warm autumn days. On warm days, you might also want to include a bottle of fresh water and a bowl or similar container to use for water. A torch is always useful to the countryman and in certain situations such as when ratting in outbuildings, essential (see Specific Ratting Gear below).

A walking stick is the countryman's "third leg": with it you can probe rat and rabbit holes (see also Whips and Things later in this chapter); hold it across a barbed wire fence as you cross it, use the handle of it to bring lower a stem of enticing-looking blackberries, test the depth of water before crossing and, of course, walk with it! A good stick soon becomes a vital part of your equipment and the day can be spoilt if it is forgotten and one has to borrow an inferior one from elsewhere. Almost any wood will do, but most are cut from hazel, no doubt because hazel is the straightest and easiest to come across. Ash is another popular choice. Undoubtedly holly makes the strongest stick and, therefore, all things being equal, lasts longest. If you take the time to look at the base of a little clump of hollies and scrape about at the base, you can often find a section growing from another that will form a very comfortable and natural handle, or even a small lump of root which once dried and shaped, will fit very comfortably in the cupped hand. I've had several over the years, all of which have become favourites due to their individual characteristics; however, as is the way of all things, they eventually get broken or lost. When out ratting, it is important not to let people get too excited and wave sticks about – it is all too easy for someone to take a swipe at a rat and a terrier be severely injured as a result.

Fig 83: A walking stick is the countryperson's "third leg"!

Still on the subject of ratting, whilst it might not be the most obvious item of useful equipment, one working terrier owner told me that he includes a bottle of washing-up liquid amongst his sundry items. Apparently, when working in farm buildings with low rafters, he squirts a line of detergent along the beams before he starts as, in doing so, he maintains that making them slippery prevents escaping rats from getting quite such a firm foothold. He assures me it works; personally, I have my doubts!

SPECIFIC RATTING GEAR
A spade, shovel and crowbar are useful pieces of equipment when out ratting. So too are gloves; not only to prevent injuries to one's hands when moving debris to allow terriers easier access, but also as a barrier against the possibility of contracting leptospirosis as a result of touching items on which rats may well have urinated. A torch – preferably a head-mounted LCD Lenser type that will keep your hands free – is essential for ratting at night or in dark farm buildings.

Arguably, the most essential piece of kit is a "smoker" of some description with which one can flush rats from their holes. Many people use an old chain saw from which its bar and chain have been removed and a short pipe and hose added to the exhaust manifold. An oil-rich petrol mix will ensure that the exhaust fumes are good and smoky! Purpose-made smokers are available

Fig 84 and 85: A "smoker" is considered by most to be a very useful piece of equipment out ratting. Photos: Greg Knight (www.www.ruralshots.com)

too. The Rat Attack Smoker Mk 2, for instance, works in the following fashion. The unit is heated by a small propane canister and uses a specially formulated fluid to generate high density smoke. As the manufacturers say, "This unit is very simple and convenient to use with many features that include hand on and off controls with self-igniting starter switch ..."

A pair of gardener's knee-pads might be a useful piece of equipment if one is intending to spend any length of time on hands and knees poking about ratting or even bolting rabbits with ferrets. They are light and easy to pack in a game bag or rucksack and will come in handy on more occasions than at first might be supposed. One enterprising terrier-man of my acquaintance has even added foam pads to the knees of his overalls (see also Overalls and Kennel Coats in What to Wear). The foam he uses is actually computer mouse pads, which are the same nylon-faced, closed-cell foam used in wet suits and are inserted into pocket-like patches sewn on the knees of the overalls. These patches are made of nylon with a Velcro closed opening at the top so the pads can be removed before the overalls are washed.

Finally, always have to hand a collar and lead as you never know when a situation might occur that will necessitate tying up your dog(s) in order to prevent either damage to themselves or to others. Whilst it is legal for your

Fig 86: Although they may hardly ever need them, all working dogs should be used to a collar and lead of some description. Photo: Greg Knight (www.ruralshots.com)

dog to be collarless whilst being used for sporting purposes, The Control of Dogs Order 1992 states that any dog in a public place must wear a collar to which must be attached a disc containing the owner's name, address and postcode. As an interesting aside, whilst hound pack members in the UK never wear collars out working, for some reason, the majority of hounds owned by the French hunts, do.

COLLARS, LEADS AND COUPLINGS

Before the Hunting Act, one of the most impressive sights ever to be seen on the hunting field was when a pack of foxhounds (often numbering 20 couple or more), could be held back with no more than a brusque word or the dangling thong of a whip whilst a terrier was entered to an earth in order to seek out the hunted fox. Once it had bolted, long-standing etiquette then insisted that it was given a certain amount of "law" before the pack could be allowed to own the line. Rarely, if ever, did any hound move before being given an appropriate signal from the huntsman and even now, in these trail-hunting days, most of the hound breeds will stand quietly when required (at a "meet", for instance), and so too will some terriers once they are experienced enough to realise that, very shortly, there is some sport to be had. Such a situation is not, however, likely to have occurred without some early basic training.

Many people cannot take their pet dog for a walk in a city park or rural countryside without the need for a lead and so the effort which results in the respect and discipline outlined above is perhaps even more awe-inspiring. Having said that, there is no shame in having a leash or two in one's pocket as there are always bound to be certain occasions where discretion is the better part of valour and one's dogs need to be brought safely to heel in a potentially tricky situation. Therefore, all sporting dogs, no matter how well they are trained, ought to be comfortable with a collar round their neck and be used to the restraints of that collar complete with leash.

Where collars are concerned, while it might be a legal requirement for a dog to wear such a thing other than when working, a micro-chip implanted into the dog's neck by a veterinary surgeon is a good idea and is far more effective than the traditional collar and name tag as, in the unfortunate event of a dog being stolen, there is a far greater chance of a dog's true ownership being proved (see also Tattoos in Kennels, Health and Hygiene).

A collar and lead is fine with one dog, but when you have a "pack" – be it as few as three or four, or as many as 30 – such restraints are impossible

Fig 87: "Couplings" have a multitude of uses. Photo: Greg Knight (www.ruralshots.com)

and are very definitely a recipe for disaster with individual leads becoming intertwined and ending up looking like a spider's web or the children's game of cats" cradle. Traditional "couplings" are the answer as far as early training of both hounds and terriers are concerned. This long-held practice is perfect for both introducing a young hound into the pack, and also in restraining the exuberance of an adolescent, potentially head-strong terrier. The method is simple and is the canine equivalent of the human expression to "attach young heads to old shoulders" as, by coupling together the experienced with the inexperienced, the youngster will learn far more quickly than it otherwise would. Couplings are also the way with which a pair of hounds or terriers is sometimes exhibited as per the schedule of relevant show classes.

<u>A word about electric collars</u>
Whilst it may perhaps be inappropriate to include the topic in a book of this nature, nonetheless, an observation or two on the subject might not be amiss. Electric shock collars are hugely popular in America and there are already some 500,000 in use in the UK. Some are designed to stop a dog from straying out of a garden whilst others are intended to shock when detonated by the owner pressing a button on a walkie-talkie-like device as a corrective measure whilst training. Manufacturers compare the current to that of a static shock, but animal charities say the technique is cruel and

inhumane and claim that dogs can tell whether they have the collar on and behave accordingly. They also fear that owners who use the collars to prevent one type of bad behaviour will be tempted to keep using them to correct other problems, no matter how minor.

Electric shock collars were banned by the Welsh Assembly in March 2010, but are still, at the time of writing, legal in England and Scotland. However, their legality is due to be debated in Parliament at Westminster and in Scotland so, as is the case with the subject of tail-docking (see Kennels, Health and Hygiene) it will be as well to keep an eye on the media and any ongoing legislation.

WHIPS AND THINGS

Whilst it is traditional to see hunt staff equipped with whips, these are never (or should never be) used to actually strike a hound and it is usually sufficient for a "crack" from it and vocal chastisement from the huntsman or whipper-in to quell any possible misdemeanour. Jack Ivester Lloyd recommended a rolled newspaper as an instrument of correction with young puppies stating that "it does them no harm and little hurt, but alarms them by its crackling noise". He did, however, like the huntsman of a traditional pack of hounds, always carry a beagling whip at exercise and in the field – but he never actually used it on his dogs: "Its purpose is to produce a 'crack!' when I want to call them back to me in a hurry. This crack gets their heads up immediately (if they are working, it is often the only thing which will) and brings them running, sterns up." In addition to his whip, Ivester Lloyd also carried a rough ash pole "shod with a thistle spud. This is an invaluable implement for digging out either rabbits or rats, and my own name for it is a 'progler' ".

Making a "cracking band"

The "crack" of a whip comes as a result of the plaited piece at the end of the thong passing through the sound barrier. You can buy what we from the north know as a "cracking band" from most saddlers and hunt outfitters or, alternatively, you can make your own with a length of baler twine or parcel string.

Take a piece of string approximately two feet (0.6m) in length and tie a small loop in one end. Hang the loop over a hook or nail and then, as close as you can to the knot of the loop, make as if to create another knot – but don't pass the end of the string right through. Keep repeating the same

Fig 88: Whips should only ever be used to warn a hound or terrier – and never, ever to physically chastise. Photo: Greg Knight (www.ruralshots.com)

action until the string has a plaited look about it and the plait is the length you require. Then, through the final loop, pass the end of the string and pull it tight. Fray the very end of the string; attach the "cracking band" through the loop of the whip's leather thong and you're all ready to begin practicing your whip-cracking technique!

HORNS AND WHISTLES

In Saxon times horns were used solely to frighten game but by the Middle Ages their purpose was both to give information and to call hounds. The French were always much fonder of the music of the chase than the British – and even today use their horns in celebration of hunting as fanfares both before and after a day's hunting – but the early English hunting had its music too, and it was far more elaborate than that of the present day when a horn is used primarily on the hunting field in order to let the followers know what is going on, and as a signal for the hounds. Generally speaking (and somewhat over-simplified for ease of explanation), the horn can be used as follows:

* One or more "toots", as a signal, e.g. (one toot) to let hounds and the Field know where the huntsman is.
* Long-drawn out notes, e.g. to indicate a blank covert, a lost quarry, or "Home".
* A succession of lively notes, as in "doubling" the horn, e.g. on viewing a hunted animal, when blowing hounds away on to the line, or at a kill.

Fig 89: Once trained, hounds and terriers will respond as well to a whistle as they will a horn.

Even with a small informal "pack", using a horn can be quite fun and most dogs of any type will respond to the horn once they understand what it is "asking" of them. It is, however, possibly more usual to find that handlers of such packs content themselves with some kind of whistle to attract their dog's attention.

Almost any proper dog whistle that you can think of was developed by the company started many years ago by Joseph Hudson – a Derbyshire farm worker who moved to Birmingham as a result of the Industrial Revolution. The "Acme Thunderer" and the "Silent Dog Whistle" are all products of Joseph's factory and are of obvious and particular use to the sporting dog-owning person. Quality and resonance is of utmost importance, as the sound emitted needs to remain constant in order to avoid confusion to the dog. Many people use a separate whistle for each of their dogs – which is all well and good when one only has two or three, but can be a trifle confusing with a large pack!

POCKET KNIVES

No country person should ever be without a penknife or pocket knife – and those of us who are country people, dog and hound owners and hunting enthusiasts cannot possibly be without one! They have many uses ranging from cutting string to tie up a fence or gate; "hocking" the back legs of a rabbit (and gutting and paunching the same); opening feed sacks; removing thorns and splinters and, if the blade is not too disgusting, cutting up a lump of cheese or slicing an apple at lunchtime!

Pocket knives should have a good blade; after all, it is its main component so you need to consider what it's made of, how it reacts under stress, how easy it is to sharpen, will it resist corrosion and how strong it is. Keep them sharp and well-oiled (unless doing so is likely to taint your cheese sandwich!).

Fig 90: A selection of knives likely to prove useful to anyone with country interests at heart.

The material used in the construction of the handle is a matter of personal choice but it should obviously be tough and resilient. Both blade and handle must "marry" together well – as one particular website says, "A quality knife designer can create something that feels like an extension of your hand."

How much a good one will cost you is impossible to say but my advice would be to get the best you can afford without it breaking the bank if you should ever unfortunately lose it. Be careful in which pocket you keep your treasured knife – I've lost far too many to mention in dog bedding and the straw of a stable as a result of them falling from my pocket, or in my gamekeeping days, by leaving them stuck in a tree or fence-post somewhere!

IDEAS FOR A FIRST-AID KIT
Make up your dog first-aid kit in a waterproof Tupperware-type container and, in indelible felt pen, write on the lid, the phone number of your local veterinary surgeon (including the one for "out-of-hours"). You should also keep this information on your mobile phone. At the bottom of the box, it might be as well to keep a small animal first-aid book and a copy of any vaccination records.

Include scissors, tweezers and a 10cc needleless syringe (to use for flushing wounds or seeds from eyes). It is also possible to buy wound staplers – but a skin "glue" might be a better alternative if it is necessary to close a wound. Add anti-bacterial wipes, sterile gauze pads and rolled bandage (preferably self-clinging). Hydrogen peroxide 3% USP (to induce vomiting and to use on infected wounds, check the expiration date from time to time and keep only fresh solution in your kit), activated charcoal tablets (effective in absorbing many toxics), antiseptic solution and an antibiotic ointment. Lanolin-based balm can also be useful for treating paw pads (see also Snow affecting pads ... in Kennels, Health and Hygiene). Also of use is an eye ointment (containing no cortisone); Styptic powder (to stop bleeding of torn toenails, etc.) and Milk of Magnesia (for certain types of poison ingestion).

First-aid box for humans
Include your own name, address and the phone number of someone to contact in an emergency. Scissors, tweezers and a sterile needle (to remove splinters). Anti-bacterial wipes or pads, sterile gauze pads, rolled gauze (bandages) and adhesive first-aid tape (in both narrow and wide strips). Sterile saline eye solution (to flush out eye contaminants and wounds), anti-histamine for bites, stings and other possible allergic reactions. Aspirin and Rescue Remedy (a natural flower essence which is available in most health food shops and can help reduce stress in both people and animals).

Some of the contents of human and canine first-aid kits such as bandages and the like are, of course, the same and it might be more practical to just make up one general kit for both yourself and your dogs. Whatever, it is also useful to include a roll of kitchen towel and some sterile gloves (failing that, help yourself to a pair or two of the type found by the pumps at a filling station!). Finally, a light nylon muzzle might not come amiss as an injured/frightened animal could very well try to bite.

KEEPING NOTES
A note-book and or hunting diary can be a very useful piece of equipment. As a diary, such a book provides a way of remembering when a visit to the vet is due; a bitch is likely to come in season, or even simply to record items of interest such as the eventual winners of a hound or terrier show. By doing so, you will begin to recognise some useful-looking dogs which may prove invaluable should you wish to breed from one of your bitches.

Ratting and rabbiting forays can also be recorded. Not only will the numbers accounted for make interesting reading in years to come, but so too will notes made of the day's experiences. Take, for example, the somewhat grumpy-sounding hunt follower of yesteryear who recorded in his hunting diary for 1935, that a day's sport had been spoilt by "children and farm stock" – he did, however, fail to elaborate further! "Dransfield", a hunting scribe at the turn of the last century was far more enthusiastic and, after a day spent visiting and hunting with the Penistone Hunt in West Yorkshire recorded in his note-book that, "... there were to be seen such a lot of fine, heavy, large-headed, long-eared, deep-tongued, black tanned and blue and dark mottled hounds as would drive any sportsman wild with delight ...'

William Scott, an enthusiastic beagle owner and rabbit hunter in America, is also keen on keeping a note-book. "I can look back through it and tell things like, what the weather was the year before; who I was hunting with; if we bagged anything, or if something funny or strange happened. I found that keeping this has actually helped me, when I get ready to go rabbit hunting. I take a quick look to see what the weather was, and how many rabbits I might have got, and where. If everything is similar, then I usually make the decision to try the same spot that day."

A note-book should be robust and long-lasting. To my mind, a Moleskine® is the answer (and, for a countryman, it's an appropriate name too!) Whilst it might not be totally waterproof, its hardback cover is of a kind that will withstand a lot of abuse and its pages are robust enough to cope with hands that might at times, be less than clean. I take a diary-sized one with me to make notes when out and about as it slips in any pocket quite easily, but there are other sizes available.

BINOCULARS

Binoculars are very definitely essential items of equipment when trail-hunting in the Fells or following hounds in some areas of Britain – in other situations they might simply be useful on occasions.

Choosing the right pair can be quite complicated and confusing but, fortunately, there is much valuable advice to be found on various Internet pages. Generally, all that is likely to be required are a pair that are easy enough to use and carry (maybe even compact enough to slip in one's coat pocket) and – most importantly – sturdy enough to ensure several seasons of hard wear and tear!

The best (most powerful) types will negate the problem of seeing a less-clear image as a result of hand-shake as you hold them up to your eyes ... and are likely to enable you to focus more clearly in poor winter light. The most common type of binocular is the "Porro Prism" (the other being a "Roof Prism") but all have a specific formula which indicates the number of times an image is magnified and also the "diameter of the objective lens in millimetres". Thus, binoculars that claim to be 7 x 35, for example,

Fig 91: A good pair of binoculars is a very useful piece of equipment at times. Photo: Greg Knight (www.ruralshots.com)

will enlarge what you are looking at seven times through a lens that is 35 millimetres. Almost all will have a coating of magnesium fluoride on the lens and this greatly helps to reduce reflection and allows more light to access.

The type of coatings vary and are identified in the following ways: "C" is the most basic; next is "FC" indicating that the lenses are fully-coated, but most readily available (and affordable) binoculars are multi-coated ("MC").

CAMERA ... ACTION!
Bearing in mind what has previously been said about sharing too many photographs on Facebook and the like (see Social

Fig 92: Photographs provide memories of a day ... and more besides.

139

Media at the very end of the Introduction to this book); a camera might not necessarily be a good idea to feature in a list of useful equipment. They can, however, like a note-book (see Keeping Notes immediately above), provide an invaluable record and happy memories of a particular day's sport.

As most mobile phones these days have a camera facility, it could be argued that a separate camera added to all the other clutter in your bag or rucksack might be an unwarranted encumbrance but, generally speaking, a camera will undoubtedly produce better results than anything taken via a mobile phone.

There are many occasions when a decent camera might be useful: following hounds, for example, when working your own dogs, to record unusual weather conditions, or a picturesque scene. You might also like to take photos for your website, to send to fellow enthusiasts in order to show them your stock, or even to submit (and possibly sell) to one of the many magazines that cater for country sports in all its guises.

SUMMER SHOWS AND SOCIALISING

ALTHOUGH it might be necessary to keep on top of the rat population no matter what the time of year and so, for those with terriers, there's always some sport to be had, for the majority, the summer months are less active in terms of actual hunting. That doesn't mean that we should sever all connections, though, and there are plenty of opportunities to keep in touch with like-minded enthusiasts during the "close" season. Local hunts are usually pretty good at organising summer events at which members and non-members alike can mix, swap experiences and, in the case of terrier shows, put their dogs before competent judges.

Many hunts have a supporters' club which followers can join and it is staggering just how successful such groups are at raising funds for the hunt. The schemes dreamt up by their committees are many and varied. There will, no doubt, be the usual things such as terrier shows, cheese and wine parties (or their equivalent), country fairs and clay shoots, but some organise inter-hunt cricket matches or even, as in the case of the Old Berkeley Beagles and Fourshire Bassets, combine to exercise hounds in the company of members and then follow that up with a barbeque and bar. A more pleasant way of fund-raising cannot be imagined!

PUPPY SHOWS
The puppy show is probably unique in being a combination of a way of saying "thank you", a social event and, to a lesser extent, a fund-raiser (see also Social Events … at the end of this chapter). In fact, as an *Observer* article commented back in 2011, "The puppy show is an essential part of a matrix of fundraising activities including quiz nights, charity auctions, balls, whist drives, garden fetes and raffles."

Fig 93: A well organized puppy show. Photo: Greg Knight (www.ruralshots.com)

Normally held in early summer when the puppies which have been out to walk have had sufficient time to readjust to their life back in kennels, the puppy show judges, usually two in number and themselves masters of hounds, will all have their own particular preference for a certain type of hound but, win or lose, all the puppy walkers for the year will be given a small token, such as a silver spoon, in gratitude for their help and assistance.

HOUND SHOWS

"Showing hounds is a serious game, but is an amusing summer game," so opined one particular master of hounds. He was right on both counts; hound shows are a serious matter and necessitate quite a few hours of hard work on the flags at the kennels if one is to be successful. The preparation usually falls upon the shoulders of the huntsman and the hounds are his responsibility when they are taken to the shows. The huntsman needs to be skilful when showing his hounds and a good one who fully understands his charges and has their trust can persuade a bad hound to show its best points. For the best results, however, he needs to enlist the help of one of the whippers-in right from the start.

A good plan is to begin with two pups, collared and leashed, and then to offer them a piece of biscuit, holding it so high that they will look upwards.

In a very short space of time it will be noticed that the puppies are standing on their toes with sterns up and necks outstretched, already in the best position for judging.

A useful tip
Sometimes the incentive offered by a biscuit is not enough and a young hound which is very shy may need a little careful handling before he feels confident enough to show himself. Such cases can often be dealt with by adopting the following procedure which, I am assured, never fails, even where general kindness and petting has met with no response.

First of all, stand over the hound with a foot on either side of him and then hold your hands with the fingers spread out so that they surround the base of his neck. Then, draw the hands upwards along the neck and head to the tip of the muzzle. Do this lightly but at the same time using a fairly rapid movement. The whole operation should then be repeated several times after which, in theory at least, it should be possible to do almost anything with your "pupil". I am assured that it even works with terriers and may, therefore, be a useful tip when considering showing them.

SHOWING TERRIERS
Originally, it was impossible to enter your terrier for a working show unless you held a Working Certificate signed by your local Master of Foxhounds saying that your dog had gone to ground in his presence at a meet of his hounds. Nowadays things have, of course, changed as a result of the 2004 Hunting Act.

Generally, show organisers include between ten and a dozen classes which cater for all the "mainstream" varieties, such as Border, Lakeland and Jack Russell types both smooth and rough. There are classes for dogs and bitches within these breeds, classes for puppies under six months, for young dogs or bitches between six months and a year, veterans over eight years and several other local "specialities" all culminating in a championship cup. Unlike the larger Kennel Club shows where it is necessary to enter the relevant classes some weeks in advance, entry to the terrier shows run by hunts, agricultural societies and clubs, can be made on the day, usually to the secretary who will be found in a small tent or the back of a horse trailer. If you are unsure as to which class to enter, ask the secretary who will be able to advise. It may even be possible to enter one dog in more than one class.

Fig 94: Terriers must be used to a close inspection from the judges! Photo: Greg Knight (www.ruralshots.com)

Showing to their best advantage

As is the case with hounds (see above), terriers can be persuaded to show themselves well as a result of a little pre-show practice at home but once in the ring, there are several points to consider. First and foremost, keep the dog on a short lead and stand as far away as practical from the next competitor – some terriers can be highly volatile and the excitement generated when several are in close proximity is often sufficient to encourage a full-scale fight!

There should be no need to pose your dog as is so often seen at the more serious shows such as Crufts. Tails do not need to be held or the legs tapped forward into a correct showing position. What is important, however, is that the dog should be used to being handled by a judge, who may wish to use the tail in order to lift up the hind quarters and assess the potential strength which is so necessary in a "working" terrier. Likewise, a judge will want to look at the dog's mouth for signs of either an undershot or overshot jaw. One final, possibly obvious point is to put the terrier between yourself and the judge(s). It is no use expecting them to be able to assess the dog's potential if it is hidden for most of the time behind the legs of the handler!

TERRIER RACING

Most organisers of terrier shows also attempt to set up a few terrier racing heats to finish off the day's events. These cannot, by any stretch of the imagination, be taken seriously and it is simply an amusing spectacle for both onlookers and competitors – and is very much a part of summer shows and socialising with like-minded enthusiasts.

Basically, a track is marked out by means of fencing or straw bales. Its length very often depends on where the event is being held but as a general guide, it is possibly a distance of around 50 metres. At one end is a block of traps, similar to those found at a greyhound stadium. At the other end is

Fig 95: And they're off! Photo: Greg Knight (www.ruralshots.com)

a winding mechanism, geared by means of cogs so that the bottom axle or spindle is going at twice as many revolutions as the hand-held turning piece at the top. A wire or rope, the same length as the course, is then fixed to the winding mechanism and, at the end closest to the traps is attached a rag or maybe even a fox's brush. This is then used to tease the terriers in the traps who will, once the doors are simultaneously lifted and the person in charge of winding in the wire or rope begins its retrieval, set off at full gallop and in an excited frenzy!

Before leaving the subject of terrier racing, whilst it is all intended as light-hearted and harmless fun, it must be mentioned that those responsible for organising such an event must make every effort to ensure that no harm can come to any participating terriers as they approach the end of the course at full speed. There have, tragically, been reports in the sporting press of dogs being injured or even killed as a result of crashing into, or becoming entangled, in the winding mechanism.

HOUND TRAILING

Hound trailing is a popular sport in the Lake District and for those that need their hunting "fix" during the summer months, they could do worse than

Fig 96 above: Hound trailing is a popular summer sport in the north of England ...
Fig 97 below: ... and can be very competitive − hence the reason that hounds have been temporarily marked in such a way that no substitutes can be made around the course! Photos: Darren Clark

visit that particular part of the world any time between April and October in order to watch some interesting – and very fast – hound work. Held mainly on weekday evenings and Saturdays, there are also hound trailing events incorporated into some of the summer fairs and agricultural shows. Those running hounds in the trails have to be members of the Hound Trailing Association, and their animals registered. Puppies are earmarked so that they can be identified (see also the subject of Tattoos in Kennels, Health and Hygiene).

The trails are laid by two people who carry rags to an agreed half-way point and they then walk away from each other, one going towards the start and the other towards the finishing point. As they travel, they periodically refresh their rags with a paraffin and aniseed oil mixture which they carry with them in plastic bottles.

Before being loosed on the trail, each hound has a coloured mark put on its head or neck by the starter in order to prevent them from being substituted half way round. (Trailing is a very competitive sport and such tricks have been tried!) As the first hounds are seen heading towards the finishing line, their owners shout, whistle, holloa and bang feed dishes (not only is it competitive, it's noisy too!). A judge and his six stewards (their main job being to catch the first six hounds) stand at the line in anticipation. Deciding which hound is the winner can be quite difficult at times and, as one judge remarked, "dead heats are surprisingly common even after a race of eight miles or so".

GAME FAIRS AND COUNTRY SHOWS

Game fairs and country shows combine many elements of a typical summer for the hunting person. Not only are they a way of keeping in touch with friends and making new acquaintances, they are an excellent showcase of what of interest is new on the market in the way of equipment, clothing and books related to a chosen sport. They are also an opportunity to enter your terriers in the appropriate show section and, quite importantly if you are part of a club or organisation, a chance to promote one's particular interest to the general public who love attending such events as part of a family day out.

Some shows and fairs include parades of hounds and terriers and this is another way of explaining to an interested public what we get up to in the winter so, if at all possible, it pays to get involved by volunteering your services in whatever way practicable. Almost all show organisers are only too pleased to have extra assistance both when planning an event and on the day itself. Most shows and fairs have their own websites nowadays and it should be possible to find the relevant contact telephone numbers and email addresses on there without too much difficulty.

Dogs left in cars at shows
Hopefully, most owners of working hounds and terriers are sensible enough not to take their animals along to a show unless they are actually competing or parading but sadly, there have been very few fairs and shows I've attended at which there has not been a call put out over the public address system saying that there is a distressed overheated dog left in a vehicle.

In common with many animals, dogs are extremely sensitive to heat, and even on a mildly warm day they can quickly overheat – even with the car windows open and water available. It is, therefore, crucial that all dog owners remember the potentially fatal consequences of leaving their dogs in the car.

To help avoid such problems, many of the larger shows and fairs offer a "canine crèche", a place where dogs can relax and stay cool, whilst being taken care of by experienced dog lovers. Caroline Kisko of the Kennel Club, says that, "These areas should aim to be relatively quiet and calming, with

Fig 98: There's always much to see (and buy!) at a country fair.

plenty of water and space for the dogs, including cages or benching ... Measures must be put into place too of course to ensure that the area is well ventilated and kept cool."

Some organisors delegate a group of volunteers to patrol the car park every hour or to check no dogs have been left unattended in cars and are in distress. Offering to help out with checks of this nature is not only obviously valuble from the distressed dog's point of view but, if done as part of your club or group's involvement with the day, is extremely good public relations.

CLAY SHOOTS AND BARBEQUES

I have always been a great believer in hunts, terrier clubs and other similar groups organising an out-of-season get-together in order that members and supporters continue to feel involved with their sport during the summer months. One of the most effective ways of doing this is to organize a clay shoot and barbeque on a suitable piece of land well away from anywhere likely to disturb (and alienate) non-hunting/sporting neighbours. To be a success, it needs to be well-planned.

Clay shoots

According to the Clay Pigeon Shooting Association (CPSA), any proposed shooting stands must include a minimum safety zone of 275 metres (300yds) in front of the general direction in which shooting takes place. Furthermore, "within that safety zone there must not be any places to which the public has access such as public highways, footpaths and bridleways, etc. Also shooting in the vicinity of overhead electrical and telecommunication cables should be avoided."

There are several different layouts possible and again, the CPSA states that, "Trap and Skeet require level ground with clear and unobtrusive backgrounds of uniform nature" while "Sporting disciplines are best suited to wooded and undulating terrain and attractive natural features are always desirable, especially water, trees, hills etc."

Some form of insurance will be required but it may be possible for recognised hunt supporter's clubs to organise extra cover for the afternoon via their existing insurance company. As to individual insurance, many of the participants will have that as part of their membership of shooting organisations such as the British Association for Shooting and Conservation (BASC). All must, of course, be in possession of a valid and appropriate shotgun certificate – or be accompanied by someone who is.

Hosting a successful barbeque
A clay shoot (and many other summer events) often culminates in a barbeque but, to be successful, it needs careful preparation, particularly if there are likely to be a good number of people in attendance – all of whom will most likely want to eat at the same time!

HUNT BALLS
Whilst they are rarely held in the summer months, probably the biggest and grandest event of a registered hunt's social calendar is the Hunt Ball. Despite the traditions associated with such an event, there is no reason at all why even the smallest "packs" of hounds and terriers should not organise their own version (see Urban Hunting: the Connaught Square Squirrel Hunt in the Sport with Your Hounds and Terriers section) and, in the early 1980s, the Bromyard Rat Hounds regularly held an annual hunt ball at the Falcon Hotel in Bromyard. Sadly, despite making enquiries, I've not been able to find out any more about this particular event – save that the venue is also used by the Clifton-on-Teme hunt for their annual ball.

Although it might be necessary to "cut your coat according to the cloth", it is always good to think big when planning a hunt ball and a decent venue is paramount. Traditionally, a ball might have been held at the local landowner's home but it is nowadays more likely that the function rooms of a hotel or a marquee might have to be hired – either of which will obviously add to the expense and reflect in the ticket prices. Food and drink are obvious essentials (some hardened hunt ball aficienados might well argue that the drink side of things is far more essentail than the food!) but other things that will make an evening successful – and profitable – are entertainments such as music and dancing, horn-blowing and whip-cracking competitions, auctions and possibly even a spoof awards ceremony.

One seasoned organiser had these thoughts: "A typical ticket price only just covers food, venue and music. The bar can make a lot of money if you are prepared to put the man hours in to run it yourself rather than get a bar company in or let the caterers do it. You've got to have a good band; it's also good to separate the music from the tables to allow wrinklies to chat!"

SOCIAL EVENTS AS A "THANK-YOU"
As well as the events run purely and simply either to raise funds or keep fellow enthusiasts in touch during the "close" season, depending on the

Fig 99: Although some Hunt Balls are still very grand affairs, it is doubtful whether many are quite as elegant as they were a century or more ago!

status of your hunt and on individual circumstances, you could do far worse than organise something as a "thank-you" to farmers, gamekeepers and the like who have helped your sport to continue in any way (see also Fostering Goodwill in Introduction).

GLOSSARY

WHILE much of this glossary is composed of traditional expressions that have been in use for many generations on the hunting field, they are still, in several instances, equally as appropriate today. They have been included both for interest, and as an explanation of what might be heard when following some of the registered and recognised packs of hounds. Other definitions featured are either "terrier-based" or in general countryside usage.

Autumn hunting:	The early part of hunting until the Opening Meet.
Babbler/babbling:	A hound that speaks when it is not hunting is said to be a babbler or babbling.
Best:	When a rabbit has given a good run or, despite all the efforts of the hounds, cannot be found again, it is said to be given "best".
Blank:	When no quarry has been found, a day is said to be "blank".
By Invitation:	This sometimes appears on the meet card of a hunt that has been invited to hunt in another hunt's country.
Cap:	A daily charge to come out hunting.
Cast:	When the hounds are looking for the line. The huntsman may cast the hounds towards where he thinks the hounds will pick it up.
Check:	When the hounds lose the line.

Chop:	When a rabbit is killed by the pack before it has had a chance to run, it is said to have been "chopped".
Clean boot:	Hunting of; the process of hunting human runners with no artificial scent applied.
Couples:	Hounds are counted in couples (i.e. one hound, a couple, a couple and a half, two couples, etc.) Couples are also two collars linked on a chain.
Cry:	Sound given from pack when hunting.
Draft:	The practice of sending a hound to another pack because it is not suitable for the pack which bred it.
Drag hunting:	Drag hunting is the hunting of an artificial scent usually on a rag dragged by a runner or rider.
Drawing:	Looking for a rabbit at the start of the hunt.
Drive:	In this instance, possibly best defined as the ability for a hunting dog to get over the ground as quickly as possible under the existing scenting conditions and not to their exclusion.
Entered:	An entered hound is a hound that has done a season's hunting.
Feather:	Hounds are said to feather or be feathering when they have the line but are unable to speak to it.
Flags:	At a show, hounds (and sometimes terriers) are shown on a small concrete or paved square known as the "flags".
Foil:	Any smell or disturbed ground which spoils the line.
Give tongue:	Noise made by hounds (or terriers) when hunting.
Heel:	Hounds are said to be hunting heel when they hunt the reverse direction to the route of the quarry.
Holloa:	In these post Hunting Act days, it is probably not necessary to "holloa" at all – but, in the interest of tradition, when the hunted quarry has been seen by a follower, he or she can holloa to inform the huntsman of the direction it has taken. It is then up to the huntsman to decide whether to lift his

	hounds to the holloa or let the pack work out the scent for themselves.
Hot bitches:	In season bitches (and not some members of the supporter's club!).
Hunt:	A hunting day usually consists of three to five hunts. Sometimes incorrectly referred to as "runs" or "lines".
Lawn Meet:	A meet where refreshments are provided by someone, usually the owner of the property where the meet is taking place.
Lift:	Taking hounds to a holloa or a view.
Line:	The scent left by the quarry.
Mixed Pack:	A pack consisting of dogs and bitches.
Mute:	A hound which hunts without speaking is mute.
Opening Meet:	The start of formal hunting each season.
Own:	Pick up the scent or line.
Rate:	Correcting hounds for some misdemeanour.
Riot/rioting:	When hounds hunt something other than that which they are supposed to be hunting, they are rioting. In the case of hounds hunting the clean boot or an artificial scent, all wildlife is known as riot.
"Runner":	A person who lays and artificial trail for hounds to follow.
Scent:	The smell, indiscernible to the human nose, left by the runners. The hounds also use the smell of the disturbed ground where the runners have been to stay on the line.
Season:	Runs from August until March. Autumn Hunting will start once the harvest is under way, usually in August and will consist of short hunts in the early morning or early evening. Formal hunting starts with the Opening Meet, usually the first Saturday in November, and will go usually to mid March.

Skirting:	When a hound or terrier cuts corners, not hunting the scent but anticipating the quarry's movements – not desirable behaviour.
Spanning:	At terrier shows, a judge will assess the chest capacity of a dog by placing his hands around the terrier's ribcage, both to check for a fair amount of lung and heart room and whether a dog is capable of fitting into an "average-sized" hole (things are obviously different since the Hunting Act 2004 and only a few people, such as gamekeepers, are legitimately allowed to work terriers underground ... and then only with certain provisos).
Speak/speaking:	Hounds do not bark; they speak, or are said to be "speaking" when they are on the line/hunting a scent.
Stern:	A hound's tail.
Subscriber:	Someone who pays an annual subscription to hunt with a pack of hounds.
Training Meet:	Another term for what has been traditionally known as "autumn hunting", i.e. the meets before the Opening Meet. Generally these hunts may be shorter.
Trencher-fed:	Hounds/terriers kept by individual hunt supporters/members and then brought to the meet by their owners for the hunting day.
View:	When followers see the quarry.
'Ware:	"Ware" is an abbreviation of "Beware" and is often pronounced "War". It simply means beware of any obstacles or potential danger such as hidden barbed wire, a ditch, or to warn hounds of livestock, rioting etc, e.g. "ware wire", "ware sheep", "ware riot" et al.

FURTHER READING

Bezzant, David: *Rabbiting Terriers: their work and training* (Crowood, 2006)
Drabble, Phil: *Of Pedigree Unknown* (Michael Joseph, 1964)
Frain, Seàn: *The Traditional Working Terrier* (Swan Hill, 2001)
Frain, Seàn: *Working Terriers: the practical methods* (Quiller, 2008)
Hancock, David: *Sporting Terriers: their form, function and future* (Crowood, 2012)
Hobson, J. C. Jeremy: *Beagling* (David & Charles, 1987)
Johnston, George: *Hounds of France* (Saiga, 1979)
Lee, Rawdon Briggs: *A History and Description of the Modern Dogs of Great Britain and Ireland* (Horace Cox, 1897)
Lucas, Captain Jocelyn: *Hunt and Working Terriers* (1931, reissued by Tide-line, 1979)
Marples, Theo: *The Sealyham Terrier* (Our Dogs Publishing Co, 1937)
Plummer, D. Brian: *The Jack Russell Terrier: its training and entering* (published privately in 1975 and then by Tideline, 1981)
Plummer, D. Brian: *Omega* (1st published by Boydell Press, 1984. New edition Coch-y-Bonddu Books, 2002)
Samuel, E. and Ivester Lloyd, J: *Rabbiting and Ferreting* (British Field Sports Society, 6th Ed, 1974)
Smith, Guy N.: *Sporting and Working Dogs* (Saiga, 1979)
Sparrow, Geoffrey: *The Terrier's Vocation* (published privately in 1949 and then by J. A. Allen, 1961)
Strawson, John: *On Drag Hunting* (J E Allen, 1999)
Taylor, Penny: *Tales from the Field: lurchers and terriers* (Skycat Publications 2012)
Various contributors: *Descriptions of the Best Terriers for Hunting* (Read Books, 2011)
Wadsworth, Waddy (and others): *Vive La Chasse: a celebration of English field sports past and present* (Dickson Price, 1989)

USEFUL WEBSITE LINKS

Association of Masters of Harriers and Beagles:	www.amhb.co.uk
Baily's Hunting Directory:	www.bailyshuntingdirectory.com
Countryman's Weekly:	www.countrymansweekly.com
Countryside Alliance:	www.countryside-alliance.org
Hounds Magazine:	www.houndsmagazineonline.co.uk
HuntingAct.org:	www.huntingact.org
Hunting Association of Ireland:	www.hai.ie
Liam's Hunting Directory:	www.hunting-directory.co.uk
Masters of Bloodhounds Association:	www.MBHA.co.uk
National Farmer's Union:	www.nfuonline.com
National Working Terrier Federation:	www.terrierwork.com
Rabbit Hunting Online:	wwwrabbithuntingonline.com
The Hunting Life, "your #1 source for fieldsports"	www.thehuntinglife.com
Vote-UK:	www.vote-ok.co.uk